THE FALL
OF A SPARROW:

Of Death and Dreams and Healing

Kent L. Koppelman

Baywood Publishing Company, Inc.
AMITYVILLE, NEW YORK

Library of Congress Catalog Number: 93-41990
ISBN: 0-89503-157-4 (cloth)
ISBN: 0-89503-158-2 (paper)

Library of Congress Cataloging-in-Publication Data

Koppelman, Kent L.
    The fall of a sparrow : of death and dreams and healing / Kent L. Koppelman.
        p.   cm.
    ISBN 0-89503-157-4. - - ISBN 0-89503-158-2 (pbk.)
    1. Grief- -Case studies.   2. Bereavement- -Psychological aspects-
-Case studies.   3. Children- -Death- -Psychological aspects- -Case
studies.   4. Fathers and sons- -Case studies.   5. Koppelman, Kent L.
I. Title.
BF575.G7K64 1994
155.9'37- -dc20   93-41990
                                                                          CIP

*This book
is dedicated
to Jason*

*who wanted to direct films
but would have taken any job
with a film company:*

"gaffer"   "best boy"

He was my "best boy"

*and to
Jan and Tess*

*Who have loved
amid the charred ruins of a family*

*And created in the ashes
like the phoenix*

A new family:

*smaller than before
but just as beautiful*

I will tell you something about stories,
[he said]
They aren't just entertainment.
Don't be fooled.
They are all we have, you see,
all we have to fight off
illness and death.

You don't have anything
if you don't have the stories . . .

from "Ceremony"
by Leslie Marmon Silko
Viking Penguin, Inc., New York, 1977.

ACKNOWLEDGMENTS

A little writing which I did just for myself eventually expanded into what has now become a book thanks to the contributions and encouragement of many people. I need to thank them for that.

For permission to use letters, photographs, and news reports, I thank Barry Duncan from the Bone and Tissue Bank, Dave Hirt of Batesville Casket Company, Margaret Kelm of the Wisconsin Eye Bank, Susan Newberry of Ellickson's Studio, Chuck Roth of WXOW-TV, Dave Fuselier and Geri Parlin of the *La Crosse Tribune,* and Judith Sinclair of the *Minneapolis Star Tribune.*

I am also deeply appreciative of those who allowed me to use their writing or their stories in this book: Steve Fink, Donald Fox, Matt Schuman, Chuck Sween, and Ray and Sue Wilson.

A special gratitude and a special debt is owed to Garrison Keillor for permission to quote from his letter, his book and his stage performance at Jason's benefit. Words cannot do justice (although I have tried) to express the mixture of respect, affection and appreciation I have (and will always have) for him.

I want to thank several people who read the manuscript and encouraged me to try to publish it: Burt and Norma Altman, Robert Bendickson, John and Julie Dryden, Craig and Sharon Fiedler, Marcia Johnson, Keith Kensinger, Loren Kucera, Wendy Lazear, Ken Maly, Donald Marshall, and William Tacey.

I must also offer a special thanks to the friends and family who helped me through the initial period of grief which made it possible for me to write this book, especially my parents, Roy and Lois Koppelman, my daughter Tess and my wife Jan. Jan and Tess contributed their stories as well as their love and support. The deepest gratitude must go to Jan who never stopped encouraging me, helping me, making suggestions, responding to changes and always, always being there. This is as much her book as mine.

Contents

PROLOGUE
The End of the Journey

Are not two sparrows sold for a farthing?
and one of them shall not fall on the ground
without your father.
But the very hairs on your head are all numbered.
Fear ye not therefore, ye are of more value
than many sparrows.

Matthew 10: 29-31
King James Version [1]

When we came down through the clouds, the first thing we saw was the Mississippi River. Tess had the window seat but the sun had sunk below the horizon and it was getting hard to see. She recognized French Island by the lights of the landing field, and soon we were on the ground. We had been gone for almost seven weeks, and we were all very tired.

Jason met us at the airport. He was standing at the bottom of the escalator with his hands stuffed into the pockets of his khaki shorts. His auburn hair looked longer, perhaps because it was damp. He wore a red bandanna around his forehead. Tess ran up to give him a hug but he wouldn't let her. I said he was too old to play the game of not wanting his sister hug him, but he said no one should get near him because he was "dirty and sweaty" from mowing the yard, vacuuming and doing a variety of chores in preparation for our homecoming.

We were anxious to see our house again, to see its high peaked roof and brick chimney silhouetted in the sky, to become reacquainted with its colors—pale blue with white trim and black shutters. It was dark by the time we drove into our garage, but there was still a sense of celebration for our "home-coming" because Jason had left on every light in the house. The light streaming through the windows beamed a brilliant welcome. Jan said it was as if a huge Christmas tree strung with large lights had magically appeared in the middle of our yard. It was good to be home.

Jason had chosen not to go to Europe with us. I had left with mixed feelings about his decision. Although I wanted him to share in our adventure, he came home deep in debt from his first year in college. Since he consistently had problems managing his finances, it seemed appropriate that he should stay home and work, although his school expenses for the coming year would be much less because he would be attending a local college. For this reason, we could afford to take him with us and I encouraged him to come, but he insisted on staying home. He said he wanted some time to himself. He had gone off to college with a desire and a dream to prepare for a career in film or television. His first year at college had been disappointing and he wanted to sort it out, make sense of it, and make plans so that next year would be better. He also wanted to be with his friends and have some fun. Last year had not been much fun.

The opportunity to take this trip arose because of my selection as one of four teachers who would offer college classes for a summer institute in Austria. Getting a salary helped to pay for the trip, but it was still an expensive proposition. Another reason for going was to see my sister in Paris. For the past year she had been working as a guide for American tourists. I hoped she would have time to take us around Paris and then we would travel on our own in France before coming home. There was a multitude of practical reasons why we should not have gone, but desire overwhelmed prudence. On the fourth of July, with Jan and Tess beside me, we watched fireworks light up the sky over Detroit through the window of an Air France airbus as we headed to Europe.

One of the consequences of Jason's decision to stay home was that we would not be here for his birthday. He would turn nineteen on July 19. I promised to call on that day, and when I did his voice sounded thick and husky, as though he had a cold. He said it was his allergies. For most of the conversation Jason talked about working on commercials as an intern for an independent television station, but he saved his most important announcement for last. He had been hired by the local ABC affiliate as a teleprompter operator for the news broadcasts. It was turning out to be a very good summer indeed.

The day after we came home Jan and I went through the stacks of mail. I was surprised to find a letter from the city "weed commissioner" informing me that his office had received complaints about the height and proliferation of weeds in my front yard. This letter was a warning that I had five days as of August 15 to cut the weeds or the city would do it at a cost of $150. Jason had mowed the yard on August 22, the day of our arrival. Although he had not met the deadline, the city had not carried out its threat. Later, some of my colleagues would ask if I had forgotten to arrange for someone to take care of the lawn while I was gone because they noticed the grass grew quite high and they said the weeds in my front yard were at least three or four feet tall.

Before leaving for Europe, I had given Jason strict instructions about his responsibilities, and one of them was the lawn. When I confronted him with the weed commissioner's letter he calmly said, "I don't do weeds." It was hard to be angry because I wanted to laugh. When I suggested that the weeds had probably aggravated his allergies he simply shrugged. I went out to work on the lawn, and I could tell by the thick stumps that the story of four foot weeds was no exaggeration. The weed stumps were so large and the roots so deep that it was hard work to dig them out. While I was digging and pulling out the roots I kept thinking about Jason's comment, "I don't do weeds."

I repeated his words in my mind several times to stir up the "righteous wrath" I wanted for the anticipated "father-to-son talk." I had used this technique before, but this time it wasn't working. I could not get angry and I began to wonder why. In the past I had often criticized Jason for qualities in his personality which I didn't like. Such criticism was based on the optimistic assumption that I could change him. In this instance, what Jason had done (or not done) was consistent with his past behavior. This was my son. Apparently I was prepared to accept him as he was. After all, the situation could have been much worse. Jason was a good person. He didn't need to be perfect. This new attitude surprised me at first, and yet I knew I was comfortable with it. Perhaps I was maturing as a parent.

As I continued working on the weeds I also wondered if my willingness to accept Jason was part of a larger "reconciliation" which had been developing during the last few years. For the first time in my life I was beginning to feel reconciled to the idea of dying. Obviously none of us has a choice about dying, but it has been difficult for me to accept the fact that I would have to die. I have contemplated my mortality since high school, not by occasional thoughts but as an ongoing awareness. I was reminded of this when I was in Switzerland this past summer, walking across a covered wooden bridge built in Luzern in the Middle Ages and looking at the images from "Totentanz" painted on panels overhead. The pictures featured a skeleton placed among people engaged in a variety of life's activities—giving birth, harvesting crops, getting married. This was a good visual representation of my awareness of death. It has been a constant presence, but not a force. It has been a cautionary influence, not a debilitating one.

During adolescence, this awareness of death steered me away from some of the reckless behavior associated with youth. Death is not real to a teenager, it is merely a possibility, perhaps a mirage. Even some adults indulge in such delusions, but for me, death was a part of everyday life. It flowed in and out like breathing. It danced to the rhythms of my heart, but I would not dance with it. I would not let it lead me around and direct the course of my life, but a consciousness of death made me more conscious of life. Being so conscious of life meant I could not imagine dying. In fact, I had refused to imagine it, until recently.

My evolving reconciliation with death did not stem from a religious experience. I consider myself a religious person, but I stopped going to church years ago because of experiences with people who claimed to be Christian. Most of these "Christians" seemed primarily interested in assuaging their own fears of death. They wanted to be comforted by a belief in a soul surviving the body, so they declared a devotion to Christ without any apparent concern for Christian commitments. Rarely did I meet anyone trying to live the beliefs Christ expressed so passionately. I wanted to express my religious beliefs in my daily life. I wanted to help people—to ease their pain, to share their joy. This was one reason I enjoyed teaching; it gave me opportunities to work with others, to be a positive force in their lives. I had been teaching for the past twenty years, and I still loved it as much as ever. Nothing extraordinary had happened to explain this change in attitude concerning my mortality.

This growing reconciliation with dying possibly stemmed from a sense of satisfaction with my life. I had achieved many goals, experienced a measure of success, received more than my share of rewards and awards. I loved and was still married to the mother of my two children and I loved my children not just because they were mine, but because they were good human beings. I had taken advantage of opportunities to travel: I had touched the Acropolis in Athens and stared in wonder at Michelangelo's ceiling in the Sistine Chapel; I stood on the rim of the Grand Canyon at sunrise and honeymooned in a rustic cabin in the Rocky Mountains; I had tasted Bavarian beer in a boisterous

Munich biergarten and drank French champagne in the shadow of
Rheims cathedral; I saw much of the finest art in the museums of
Vienna, New York, Amsterdam, Chicago and Paris. And more. For
someone who had grown up as one of ninety people in a Nebraska
village called Winnetoon, I felt fortunate to have had such a life.

Feeling grateful for the richness of my life, my unwillingness to
accept not being in the world seemed almost indecent, a kind of ingratitude or immaturity. I once read that the environmentalist John Muir
claimed to be richer than J. P. Morgan. When challenged to prove his
claim he said he had all the money he wanted but Morgan didn't. This
was how I felt about my life. It seemed selfish to wish for more. It was
reasonable to hope for more of the same, but "the same" would suggest
a repetition of what I had already experienced. This conclusion created
a comforting vision of the future, but not an exciting one.

Perhaps this is the curse of contentment—to be satisfied with what
you have is to be resigned to a pleasing, but predictable life. At least
dying would provide a different kind of experience, whatever that
might be. It began to seem possible that I could actually accept such an
idea, that I could regard death as an adventure instead of a fearful
finality. What I didn't know was that my contentment was about to be
shattered.

*   *   *

*My wife and I were in our car on the way to meet some friends.
I parked on the shoulder of the road before an unfamiliar wooden
bridge. Jan and I got out of the car and began to walk over the bridge
which arched like a rainbow high above some railroad tracks. The
bridge was ancient. The wide, thick wooden planks had warped and
buckled over time, making our passage across it more than a little
treacherous.*

*As Jan and I reached the peak of the arch and began to descend,
I noticed a boy standing on the other side of the bridge. The boy
stood motionless next to a withered tree in a clay pot. The tree was
about as tall as the boy, perhaps four feet, with a few scrawny
branches and not a single leaf. The boy said nothing. He was dressed
in clothes a little too large for him and he wore a cone shaped hat.
I wondered if he was trying to sell the tree or what other purpose he
might have for being there. His image disturbed me. We walked past
him to the street and made our way to a restaurant housed in a catwalk
spanning the street.*

We enjoyed a good meal and good wine and had an animated conversation with the friends who met us there. Occasionally I looked out the large glass windows to the street below. There were no cars, not even a pedestrian. When we left, Jan and I retraced our steps to the wooden bridge. We were both a bit "giddy" from the wine, not quite inebriated, but lighthearted and laughing. As we walked up the ascending slope, the bridge seemed even more treacherous than I remembered. In addition to the warped and uneven planks, some planks were missing, leaving gaps large enough for a person to fall through. I sobered up quickly at the sight, but Jan did not seem affected by it. I was determined to be careful for both of us since Jan did not appear to recognize the seriousness of the situation.

As we walked toward the peak of the arched bridge, I was distracted for a moment by the sight of the boy. There he stood, unmoved and unmoving, in the same place by the same barren tree. Once again I wondered who he was and what he was doing there. I assumed he must be an "orphan," and pitied him. I turned to say something to Jan but she had walked ahead of me while I paused to stare at the boy. I was terrified to see her walking toward one of the huge gaps in the bridge planking. I ran ahead and grabbed her hand to pull her back. I was almost breathless from fear, but Jan merely giggled and said she had to sit down. She walked over to the handrail, a simple construction of boards nailed to the top of the wooden posts placed at regular intervals. Another line of narrower boards was nailed to the middle of the posts.

When Jan reached the handrail, she sat down on the edge of the bridge, leaned under the middle line of boards and then sat up facing me with her legs straight out and her arms bent in front of her on top of the boards. She put her chin on her arms and smiled, but it made me nervous to see her sitting there with nothing behind to keep her from falling. I said she shouldn't sit there and walked toward her. Suddenly her smile faded and her eyes took on a glazed look that seemed a mixture of dullness and acquiescence, as though she had just remembered an unexpected and unpleasant experience. She brought her knees up to her chest and in that moment her face disappeared as she fell backwards. It almost seemed as if she had intended to do so.

Fear made my heart beat faster as I crept toward the edge of the bridge. I tried to believe that there was a ledge just out of sight under the edge of the bridge. I tried to imagine Jan's face appearing suddenly over the edge, smiling at me. But as I came closer to the edge, hesitating, giving her time to play out the "joke," nothing happened. I stopped. I *knew that her face was not going to appear, that if I looked over the edge of the bridge I would see her body lying broken and bloody on the railroad tracks below. Just thinking of that sight sickened me. I could not force myself to look.*

*   *   *

I woke up.

I told Jan about the dream. I was shaken by it. She just grinned and said, "You're always trying to get rid of me in your dreams." I had to smile. She was right. Similar nightmares had disturbed my sleep in the past, and I always awoke with anguished feelings of fear and loss, but this dream was different. It was more vivid than any previous dream and much more elaborate in detail. I knew it must mean something, and I distinctly felt that it was a warning of some kind, but it was too ambiguous. For some time afterwards I thought about the dream and tried to decipher a meaning, but I was not successful. Although I could not understand it, it continued to haunt me.

CHAPTER 1

In the Dark of Night

No, it shall not be. You cannot die . . . Such things cannot be . . . If so, then everything is a snare, the earth, the sky, the infant's cradle, the mother's bosom, the human heart, love and the stars! God would be a traitor, and man a dupe! And nothing would be left! Creation would be insulted! And all would be a yawning abyss! [2, pp. 252-253]

Victor Hugo
The Laughing Man

The call came shortly after 11:00 at night. Must be friends calling long distance, I thought, waiting until the rates went down. Jan answered it. Fear on her face as she came breathlessly back to the living room. It was the Houston County Sheriff. There had been an accident. It was serious. Jason.

Jason. My son.

The sheriff was calling from his car phone. It must be bad.

Should we wake Tess?

It's late and she has school tomorrow. Let's wait.

The hospital is nearby. We can run over there and see what the situation is and then one of us can come back for Tess.

We hurried to the car and drove to the hospital only five minutes away. The ambulance was pulling into the parking lot as we arrived. We knew it was Jason. We followed it and parked in the lot while the ambulance backed up to the doors of the emergency entrance. Jan was

1

running to the ambulance. I walked quickly, trying to be calm. The paramedics would not let Jan see Jason.

He's pretty bad, they say.

The doctor's waiting for him, they say.

Please go into the waiting room, they say.

Barely breathing, trying for a glimpse of Jason as they wheeled the stretcher away, Jan and I were taken through a public waiting area into a private room. No one would tell us how bad it was. Fear struggled with anger. In a bitter, hurting voice I heard myself say to a nurse, "I wish they would at least tell us if he's alive." I don't remember the nurse's response.

Jan said she was feeling sick. She went to the bathroom. Within minutes a doctor came in and seemed ready to explain the situation, but then she asked where my wife was. I explained and the doctor left saying she would be right back. I was irritated with Jan for not being there. Waiting was agonizing; I felt an overwhelming sense of desperation; I felt helpless. I was trying not to think the worst. I prepared myself for statements like "He is in critical condition," or "He's sustained . . . (some serious injury)." Sustained seemed like a good word to me, any word would do if it meant Jason was still alive. I needed such a word to help me breathe again.

Jan returned, pale and distraught, and within seconds the doctor was back. I cannot remember how she began, but I cannot forget the last four words ". . . he didn't make it."

My son is dead.

My body felt like electric shocks were running through it as I stiffened and threw my head back and groaned. It sounded heartrending to me and I stopped until I remembered whose heart had been ripped apart and the pain swept over me. Again I stiffened and groaned, more loudly than before, as large tears poured down my cheeks. My eyes were closed. I could not hear Jan or the doctor or the nurse. I knew that if I opened my eyes I would be unable to see because my eyes were too full of tears. A quiet voice within advised me to comfort Jan, but that voice was quickly drowned out in a roar of pain louder than a waterfall.

I had no sense of time; I did not know how much time had passed before my groans softened and I could hear muffled sounds coming from Jan and the doctor. I began to distinguish the doctor's voice as she calmly explained that Jason had suffered massive head injuries. He had died instantly. There was nothing they could do. They would have him ready for us in a few minutes if we wanted to see him.

Yes, we want to see him.

While we were waiting, the nurse asked if we wanted to talk to the paramedics who had brought Jason to the hospital. We did. As they spoke to us they mentioned a young man who worked with Jason and was driving behind him when the accident happened. He had seen Jason being thrown from the car and he knew Jason must be seriously injured. He stopped and found Jason and gave him CPR. By the time the paramedics arrived they could find no pulse. They were sure Jason died instantly. The social worker asked if we would consider donating his eyes to the eye bank, and if they could take some bones and skin tissue. We agreed. She said the nurse would talk to us about this later.

Finally we were taken through the public waiting area and down a corridor to the room where they had wheeled him on the stretcher. Someone had put a blue paper shower cap over his head to hide his injuries. A sheet covered his body except for his arms. They had cleaned off most of the blood except for some caked around his fingernails. He looked pale, bloodless, but his face was almost unmarked. Jan went to his right side. On the way down the corridor one word had been throbbing through my mind — "Lazarus." As I walked over to Jason's left side and reached for his hand, I desperately wished for a miracle. His hand was cold. I squeezed it as hard as I could in the hope that some of my warmth could be transferred to him. I just stood there, squeezing and hoping for several minutes. Then I had to walk away from the body, and for the first time his death became real to me.

For a long time I would alternate between being conscious of Jason's lifeless body and wanting to waken from this nightmare.

When I turned back to his body, I noticed Jason's hair poking out at the neck from beneath the blue shower cap. The beautiful auburn hair was a little long, and it looked redder because it was wet, much as it looked that day at the airport. (*At the airport, when he was alive.*) I pictured people washing his hair to get rid of the blood. Soft moaning sounds passed through my lips. I watched Jan kiss Jason's cheek. So much pain. I gently pulled the sheet down to see and touch his broad, hairless chest. He was a big boy, not a man yet, not ever now. There were a few scratches and bruises. There were pads on his chest. I wondered what their purpose was:

Is this what they use when the heart stops?

Did they try to restart his heart?

How do I restart my heart?

I feel so tired.

Jan stood there, on the other side of our son's body, but there was nothing we could do for each other. We were sharing the same experience but we could not share our reaction to it. No words could express what either of us were feeling, so there seemed no point in speaking. And as for consoling each other, that would have to wait. My legs quivered. All that was keeping me upright was numbness. The numbness in my brain took the form of a mild buzzing, like static on the radio with the volume turned low. I felt numbness and pain at the same time, and I knew the numbness masked even more pain. I was grateful for it because I could not imagine enduring any more pain than I already felt.

At times I had to turn away from Jason's body, but I kept coming back to touch it, because it was all I had left of him and I knew the time was short. It was only his body. I knew that. He was too pale, too cold, too still to be alive, but I knew the next time I saw him he would be even more transformed by mortician's makeup. This was the closest he would ever come to the way he looked when I last saw him, when he was alive. So I had to look. I had to touch, despite how cold he felt. I had to kiss his cheek and tell him how much I loved him, even though I knew his ears could not hear me.

Time passed. Jan looked at me. We were thinking about Tess. We had to decide what to do.

We have to wake her up and tell her.

Could you keep the body here for a while longer?

We might be coming back with our daughter.

We don't know for sure.

We will call you as soon as we talk to her.

They said they would keep the body in the room until we called to tell them if we were coming back or not. The nurse once again asked about donating Jason's eyes to the eye bank. They could not take his organs. Once a person has died, the organs cannot be used for transplants. They would be able to use his eyes, the bones from his legs and some of his skin tissue for skin grafts. We signed the papers giving permission to do this. We were introduced to the Houston County Sheriff. He repeated what we had already heard, that there was nothing he could do, that he was sorry. He pointed to Jason's L.L. Bean backpack on the floor. He found it in the car so he put all of Jason's "personal effects" in it. Jan walked over and picked up the backpack. Finally, we left the hospital and drove home.

The lights were on downstairs but upstairs, where Tess was sleeping, it was dark. She was still asleep. As I walked up the steps to Tess's room, I turned on the light and called out her name. She answered clearly, but I could tell that she had been asleep. I began by saying we had some bad news. Tess sat up in bed and Jan sat next to her. We tried to keep the explanation simple. There was an accident. Jason was on his way home from work and the car went off the road. He didn't make it. Jason was dead. Tess was stunned for a few seconds, unable to respond, then she burst into tears and Jan hugged her and whispered to her while I silently wept. After a few minutes, rubbing her eyes with her hands, Tess cried out, "Why does my brother have to be dead?" We had no answer for her. There was no answer.

After a while, we asked Tess if she wanted to go to the hospital to see Jason. I said his face was not cut or bruised and that he might not look very "natural" at the funeral, but it was her decision to see him now or to wait. She wanted to see him now. She got up to get dressed and I went downstairs. I called Jason's friend, Matt. Although it was late, I knew he would not be asleep. Matt answered and I told him what had happened. I could tell from his voice that he could not believe what I was saying. It was not real to him. It was too real to me. He offered to call some of Jason's friends and I thanked him. Jan and Tess came downstairs and we drove back to the hospital, back to the room, back to the body.

Jan and I went right to Jason's body as soon as we entered the room and began touching him, caressing him. We were not thinking about what we were doing. We simply knew that we would never be able to do this again. Tess stood apart and stared, tears running down her cheeks. After a while she came closer. She began touching Jason's arms, tentatively. Her expression was a mixture of curiosity and awe. Jan was kissing Jason's cheek, his lips. Time passed. Tess said, "I want to give him a hug. He wouldn't let me hug him when he was alive." She grabbed Jason's arms and leaned her head down on his chest. It was a slight hug. Jason wouldn't have objected.

Time passed. Jan and I were still touching, looking, weeping, hurting. The staff had said "Take as long as you want," but I knew they were waiting for us. Tess was ready to go. It was late. But it was hard to let go of Jason, literally as well as figuratively. This was no ordinary leave-taking. I didn't want to let go and yet I knew we must. Jan and I looked at each other. Without speaking we both knew it was time to go. We looked at Jason one last time, one last touch, one last kiss, and then we shuffled toward the door. We thanked everyone on the way out and then we were outside in the quiet darkness, walking away from the bright lights of the hospital and into the semi-darkness of the almost deserted parking lot.

At home, we sat in the living room and talked. Tess wanted to go to school tomorrow, but Jan told her not to set her alarm. After she was awake we could discuss whether or not she still wanted go. Jan took Tess upstairs to bed. I needed to call someone, but it was so late. I thought of my sister in California. It was two hours earlier there, so it was only a little after midnight. When she answered the phone I immediately told her what had happened. It was as though I needed to say the words for the first time, to convince myself that this horrible thing was true. It helped a little to talk about it, but it did not ease the pain. I knew I would not be able to sleep so talking gave me something to do. Jan suggested that I call my younger sister in Paris. It was early morning in France. I dialed the number and someone answered and soon I heard my sister's voice. We talked for a short time and we wept together.

After this second call I began to feel exhausted, but still not sleepy. It was 3:00. Jan and I needed to get some rest. It would be a long day tomorrow. Once in bed it was obvious that sleep would not come. We were tired but restless, full of feelings but unable to speak, tortured by visions from the hospital, images of the accident, questions we could not answer.

Suddenly we heard the phone ringing in Jason's room. Jan jumped out of bed to answer it. It was Matt. He forgot that he was calling on

Jason's line. He just wanted us to know that he had called most of Jason's friends. He wanted to see Jason, but Jan wasn't certain that the hospital staff would let him. That was all. I looked at Jan as she lay next to me, silent. After a few minutes, she started to talk. When the phone rang, she hoped it meant she had been dreaming and was now awake. We were both beginning to realize that there would be no "awakening" from this nightmare. It was real.

Minnesota crash fatal for motorist

LA CRESCENT, Minn. — A 19-year-old La Crosse man was killed Wednesday night as the result of a one-car accident on a town of La Crescent highway.

Jason D. Koppelman, 1017 West Ave. S., was eastbound on Hwy. 25, near La Crescent, when he lost control of his car and was thrown about 80 feet, according to a spokesman for the Houston County Sheriff Department.

Koppelman was taken by Tri-State Ambulance to Lutheran Hospital, La Crosse where he was pronounced dead.

The sheriff department is investigating the accident.

Reprinted with permission from *La Crosse Tribune*, September 14, 1989, La Crosse, Wisconsin.

Remembering . . .

Lying in bed, I knew I would not sleep. I tried not to think about anything, but I kept thinking about Jason. How could he be dead? He was so young, so alive, so full of promise. I remembered the day Jason left for college, full of enthusiasm and high expectations. He had chosen the University of Iowa because of their film program, but he also had fond memories of the small town near Iowa City where he spent three years of his childhood. In addition, one of my sisters lived in Iowa City, so Iowa seemed the perfect choice. It didn't turn out that way.

The problems began with an obnoxious roommate, but Jason was even more frustrated that he could not take courses in his major and he found it difficult to get interested in his classes. He had not been conscientious about getting assignments in on time in high school, and he continued this pattern at college with even harsher consequences. Jason seemed to feel better after his roommate moved out, but he was experiencing the feelings of isolation, loneliness and homesickness which are common to young people away from home for the first time.

Why was I thinking about all of this? Perhaps because it was my normal way of thinking about Jason, a living Jason and not the cold body I had touched at the hospital. I could not think of my son as dead. I remembered when he called to say he wanted to transfer to the University of Wisconsin, but he had missed the deadline. This was so typical of Jason. We discussed his options. He decided to transfer to Viterbo College where Jan worked. Although he would lose some credits, he could finish his core requirements and try to bring up his grade point average before transferring to the University of Wisconsin. He was a little disappointed about leaving Iowa, and even more disappointed when he discovered that he was still classified as a freshman at Viterbo. He seemed to take it well, but I was surprised to hear what one of the college counselors said to Jan.

This counselor was involved in freshman orientation. He always concluded his remarks to any group of freshmen by emphasizing the importance of developing good study habits, and after that he would ask each student to make a comment or ask a question. When he met with Jason's group and it was Jason's turn to talk, he told the group that the counselor had given them good advice about studying. He confessed that he had just spent the previous year at the University of Iowa, but at Viterbo he was " . . . a freshman, again." The counselor was impressed that Jason had the courage to say this in front of his peers, and the look on their faces suggested that his comment had made an impact.

It was hard to believe. I had never known Jason to do something like this. Throughout his adolescence Jason had tried to hide from people, to be invisible. I think he hoped to avoid the bullies and cruelties of the world; of course, it didn't work. Suddenly here was a Jason who spoke openly of his failure, risking vulnerability in front of strangers. What was happening? Why was he willing to take such a risk? Jason was obviously changing, and it was exciting to think about what sort of person he was becoming.

I kept thinking about Jason, trying not to think about his death, trying to keep a living image in my mind a while longer. I remembered when he came to the house for lunch two weeks ago and told me about his unsuccessful attempt to go on a diet this past summer. He had made an appointment with a doctor. As Jason was growing up, he also grew out. By his seventeenth birthday he was large—six feet tall with a broad chest, round face, large hands and feet. He knew he was overweight because of his poor eating habits, but he also knew he did not have the will power to change. If an authority figure provided explicit instructions on what to eat and strict orders to follow those instructions, he was convinced that he would "stick to it" and lose weight.

Unfortunately, the doctor Jason encountered was not the crusty autocrat he had in mind, but a modern doctor who kept asking Jason what he wanted. The doctor was trying to get Jason to take responsibility for his eating choices, but given a choice, Jason would eat as much as he wanted of whatever he wanted whenever he wanted. That was how he became overweight. Since this was not a good strategy for losing weight, Jason wanted the doctor to provide the plan. The doctor kept asking Jason what he wanted and Jason kept saying "I don't know, what do you want me to do?" Since the doctor kept repeating his question and wouldn't prescribe a plan, Jason finally left in utter frustration.

Jan was glad that Jason wanted to lose weight and urged him not to give up. Jason said he "kind of" blamed his parents for his poor eating habits. Since we liked to indulge in food and drink whenever we felt like it, our behavior encouraged him to do so. "After all," he said, "I really look up to you guys." I mentioned several other habits I "indulged in" which Jason did not imitate, like regularly reading for pleasure, being frugal with money, and picking up after myself. Unless Jason could prove that he was influenced by these positive behaviors, I wasn't willing to take responsibility for being a negative role model on that one issue. Jason grinned and blushed. He didn't argue the point, but he did repeat his concern that Jan and I should take better care of ourselves saying, "I think a lot of you." For the second time, in a self conscious way, Jason was saying he loved us.

Although the argument had been playful, his expression of love was sincere. We never doubted his affection, but it had been a long time since Jason had said he loved us. When he came home from college at Christmas, he tried to say it in a curious, nonverbal way. He would walk up to Jan or me and suddenly drop his forehead down on our shoulder, almost like a head butt. We told him he was being strange, but he only responded with a goofy grin. One time Jan asked if he really wanted a hug. He only shrugged, but he didn't try to escape when she put her arms around him. Now he was trying to express himself verbally. He was changing, maturing, and it was a pleasure to hear those words of love.

I did not see Jason on Wednesday, the day of the accident. I had seen him the day before. He had only been at Viterbo for two weeks but he was pleased with his courses and his teachers. He had started his job as teleprompter operator for newscasts at the television station. He was excited about his first article for the student newspaper and he was planning to ask the editor if he could be assigned to write movie reviews. He seemed to enjoy dorm life, if not dorm food. Of course, he could always raid our refrigerator, which happened quite often.

On Tuesday Jason came home to take a shower before going to work. I was in the kitchen working on a report. Since the bathroom with the shower was off the kitchen, I saw Jason go in and out. He wore a plain brown shirt but he had wrapped a brightly colored Hawaiian beach towel around his waist. Shortly after he had gone upstairs I went up to get some papers I had left by the computer. As I walked upstairs I heard music coming from the "guest room." Walking by the open door I could see he was watching a music video on television. Then I saw Jason. He was prancing around in front of the television set, still wearing the orange and yellow beach towel wrapped around him like a skirt. I had to smile. It was good to see him happy, so happy he just had to dance! I knew he would be embarrassed if he saw me watching him, so I quickly walked past the door and searched for the papers.

Jason must have heard me because he stuck his head through the door. With a sheepish grin he asked what I was doing. I pretended to be very busy and merely mumbled that I was looking for some papers. I think he believed that I had not seen him. Walking downstairs, I smiled as I recalled that image of Jason dancing his joy, the joy of being alive. It was a special image for me because this was the part of Jason I had always loved dearly. It was the part of him which had been battered by some of his adolescent experiences. Perhaps he was preparing to reclaim that part of himself. I hoped so. He was obviously happy at Viterbo, and that made me happy. This brief scene was the last time I saw him alive, but that image will always be a vivid memory. At any moment I can close my eyes and see Jason, the orange and yellow beach towel wrapped around his waist, dancing.

My mind raced through memories which reflected the person Jason was or the person he was becoming. Many memories simply recalled ordinary, mundane encounters. While I was remembering, so was Jan. During that night and for several days and nights thereafter she remembered the times she had seen Jason during the past few weeks and especially the last few days. Later we would talk to each other about those experiences. She had more opportunities to see Jason since some of his classes were in the same building as her office. She had even written his schedule of classes on her calendar so she would remember when he had free time. Jason had classes from nine until noon on Mondays, Wednesdays and Fridays, so he would usually stop by during the afternoon. This was when she saw him on Wednesday, his last day.

On Tuesday I had made some oatmeal raisin cookies in the evening and brought them to my office the next day. Jason didn't look in after lunch as he had been in the habit of doing, and I wondered if he was working in the computer lab. He had an article due that day for the college newspaper and I suspected that he had waited until the last minute to finish it. While doing an errand, I stopped in at the computer center and saw him working on the article. I mentioned the cookies and he said he was almost finished and promised to stop by later.

When he came, I was busy interviewing students who had applied for work/study positions. Jason came into the office and flopped in my chair. He was wearing the white button down shirt I had bought him for the pizza delivery job last summer, and a pair of recently purchased khaki shorts, but no matter what he wore, his clothes always looked much older than they were. He also wore his favorite dilapidated gray (originally white) canvas sneakers (no socks) which he had propped up on my desk as he tipped back in my chair—a typical pose.

When I finally had a chance to talk, Jason asked if I would proofread his article (he was a terrible speller). I was pleased that he wanted to show me his article, but I didn't have much time. I glanced at it quickly and made a few suggestions, but then I had to interview another student. Jason left a few minutes later saying he had to drop off the article at the press room before going to work that night. He didn't even blush when I said "Goodbye sweetheart." I guess he had finally gotten used to me calling him "sweetheart" in front of people. Perhaps he recognized that he had to accept such behavior from "crazy old mom."

It was 4:45 when I got home from work that day. I was surprised to see Jason's car still parked in the alley behind our house. He was supposed to be at work at 5:00 and it took about 15 minutes to drive there, but then Jason, like his father, tended to be at least 5 minutes late for everything. Had he stopped to eat supper before going to work? I walked over to his car. He was just taking a plastic container of windshield wiper fluid into the garage. The indicator light had come on so he had stopped to add some fluid. Another "goodbye" (without the "sweetheart" this time) as he jumped in the car and drove away. That was the last I saw of him.

CHAPTER 2
The Mourning After

Yes the world is the best place of all
                    for a lot of such things as . . .
making babies and wearing pants
                    and waving hats and
                    dancing
                and going swimming in rivers
                    on picnics
                in the middle of the summer
                and just generally
                    'living it up'

                Yes
but then right in the middle of it
                    comes the smiling

            mortician [3, pp. 88-89]

Lawrence Ferlinghetti
A Coney Island of the Mind

After a sleepless night, Jan got out of bed and went downstairs. I heard her speaking softly. I looked at the clock. It was 6:30. I sat up on the edge of the bed. I guessed that Jan had begun the first hard task we would have to do today, making phone call after phone call to family and friends to tell them what had happened. I felt sluggish. I couldn't decide what to wear. I tried to think of words to say. Jason was killed in an accident. Such words made knots in my stomach and throbbed through my mind.

I went downstairs and made some coffee. Jan suggested that I call my sister in Iowa and ask her to call my parents. Jan had already called her brother in Omaha and asked him to call her father. It was simply too painful to think of talking to our parents about Jason's death. We alternated as we made our calls, pausing in between to cry, to console each other, to ache. We heard our voices repeating the same words like a litany—"there was an accident," "Jason drove off the road," "He didn't make it." Jan's father called but could hardly talk. "Why couldn't it have been me," he moaned. My mother and father called. They were calm and consoling and talked bravely until my father said, "We all kind of expected great things out of Jason." Then he burst into sobs and my mother could not speak. I heard a "click" and then the dial tone.

We called to explain why we would not be at work today; we called Tess's school to explain her absence; we called family and friends. Each call took its toll on our emotions and our energy. We remembered to call some of Jason's friends to ask if they would be pallbearers. We tried to think of other tasks. I began to notice how often I stood rubbing my hands together as though washing them or rubbing both hands back and forth on my forearms, restless habits borrowed from my father.

By late morning we had completed most of the calls, and people began to call us. They offered their help, their sorrow, their love. The doorbell rang as people came by with thoughtful gifts: some food; an embrace; a comforting word. Tess came downstairs. She fixed breakfast for herself and ate while Jan and I responded to the phone or the doorbell. Tess still wanted to go to school. Jan and I realized that the people calling and coming by were focusing their attention on us. We were sure that Tess would get support and sympathy from her teachers and her friends. I drove her to school and told her to call if she wanted to come home.

It was quiet in the house when I returned. No one called or came for a time, so Jan and I sat in the living room and tried to talk. I wanted to say something which I knew would sound crazy but I needed to say it. I talked about having another child. Would that be possible? Could we do that? Jan wondered if I wanted a child to replace Jason. I didn't know; I didn't think so. What I did know was that we were good parents and had raised our children with love. I had always wanted a boy and a girl. I wanted to watch them become adults and start their own families and give me grandchildren to love. Now my boy had been taken from me. Having another boy would not replace Jason, but would give me a second chance to have a son to love. Jan reminded me that she was forty two, and there would be serious risks for her and for the baby if she were to have a child at her age. She was right and I was sorry I asked. It was a desperate attempt to relieve the oppressive sense of helplessness.

By the afternoon, the first flowers came. I showed them to Jan and read the card aloud. For some reason, these flowers pushed us both over an emotional edge. We had been calm for several hours as we talked with people who called or came to the house, but now our eyes welled up with tears. We went to different parts of the house to weep alone, unable to console each other. I tried to think of some greater good which might come from this tragedy. I could think of none. Sometimes a death, although tragic, brought families together, caused people to re-examine their lives, served as a catalyst for the bereaved to pursue a cause or to seek some redress for an injustice, but there was none of that here. From what we had been told, Jason was driving a little too fast, probably in a hurry to get home. For some reason he drove onto the shoulder of the road as he approached a curve. The car went into the ditch and tumbled end over end and he was killed. What "greater good" could come of this?

Throughout the morning I tried to think of good things, to remember our years with Jason and to make a mental list of all the things for which Jan and I should feel grateful:

> He was with us for nineteen years.
> He knew that we loved him.
> He knew that he could always count on us.
> He was developing into an adult who was caring and conscientious.
> He started college this year with enthusiasm and optimism.
> He seemed happier these last few weeks than he had been
> for a long time.

But all of this was meaningless in the bitter context of his death.

Luigi Pirandello wrote a story entitled "War" which described a mother and father taking a train to the front to be near their only son [4]. They met other parents of soldiers on the train. Some of the parents began to engage in a lively argument about whether it was worse to lose an only son or to lose a son when you had another at home whose presence would be a constant reminder of the son who died. The mother became distressed by such talk. One man began to speak enthusiastically about his son who died fighting for the fatherland. He told of the glory his son achieved and boasted that he wouldn't have it any other way. Confused by his exuberance, the mother asked, "Then . . . is your son really dead?" Surprised by the question, the man could find no words to reply. At last he broke into "harrowing, heart-rending, uncontrollable sobs." [4, pp. 257-258]. I had always appreciated the power of that short story, but it offered me no consolation. It simply described a reality I had been forced to live.

Part of this reality was to take care of the various duties which death requires. I called the mortuary a few blocks from our house to arrange for the funeral. I also called Keith, a minister from my campus, to ask if he would conduct the service. Jan and I met with the funeral director to discuss the details and Keith joined us. We provided the funeral director with the information needed for the newspaper obituary. He asked if we could give him a photograph of Jason for the obituary and another for the mortician. I hadn't thought about photographs, but Jan had brought several copies of Jason's high school graduation pictures.

Jan and I reviewed the musical selections available (on tape) for the public visitation and the funeral. The music was mostly religious, hymns that Jason would not have known nor liked. What he liked was music from movies. Jan suggested that we ask Jason's friend Matt to record some of Jason's favorite movie themes for the visitation. We didn't know what to do for the funeral. Finally, I selected "In the Garden" because it was one of my favorite hymns, and Jan selected "Amazing Grace" because she knew it was used in a movie Jason liked.

Keith needed to know what verses we wanted him to read from the Bible, but Jason did not have favorite Bible verses. He had only started to read the Bible with interest recently. I asked Keith to make that decision since it was not really for Jason but to offer comfort to others. Did we want anything else in the service? We didn't know. It was hard to think. Keith said there was no need to make all of these decisions today, but he would come to our home tomorrow to discuss the final details. We would have to complete the details of the service at that time so the mortuary had time to print the funeral programs.

More questions. What did we want to do with the money people were sending? Jan suggested that the money could go to a local foundation which provided college scholarships. When Jason graduated from high school, he had received one of these scholarships. It came at a time when he was feeling insecure about whether he would be able to achieve his goals for the future. The letter announcing his selection as a recipient of a scholarship produced a dramatic change in his attitude. It was as though someone other than his parents had said they believed in him.

The funeral director also asked what cars should be lined up behind the hearse and in what order. Although Jan and I told him the names of the friends and relatives who were coming, we couldn't remember what kind of car they owned. More questions. At last we were taken down to the basement to select a casket. This was one of the hardest tasks. Jan and I wandered around a room full of coffins like children lost in an ominous forest. How do you "shop" for a coffin? What criteria do you use? Jan thought metal coffins looked like cars without windows. We selected an oak coffin.

The cemetery we had chosen was close to my campus. We drove there to talk to a woman about available gravesites. How many lots did we want? Another decision. Would Tess understand that if we only bought three it was not to exclude her? Would she understand our purchase of three lots as an expression of hope that she would not die young like her brother but would go to college and work and marry and have children and be buried elsewhere? The woman assured us that if we bought four lots we could always sell the fourth lot to someone else or sell it back to the cemetery if we did not need it. We bought four lots.

We were shown burial lots in the new section of the cemetery, but it was flat and treeless. Jan asked if there were four lots together somewhere else. We were taken to the edge of the old section to a spot with trees shading it. We liked it much better. We were told we didn't have to pay for the lots today; the purchase price would be included with the bill we would receive from the mortuary.

When Jan and I returned home, Tess was talking to some of our friends. Most family members couldn't come until tomorrow except for Jan's two brothers who would arrive that evening. Although I appreciated the thoughtfulness of our friends, I also felt like being alone. Part of me enjoyed the pleasant conversation but part of me did not want to smile or laugh or act as though everything was normal. These conflicting emotions confused me. I didn't know what to do. It would take time to realize there was nothing to do. There is no way to prepare yourself for the death of your child.

Some consolation came from surprising sources. I received a phone call from a woman who identified herself as Marilyn. She said I did not know her but we had a mutual friend who had told her of the accident. Her son, also named Jason, had been killed in a car accident two years earlier. He was sixteen. He had been to a party with some friends and was on his way home when the accident occurred. The gas tank exploded and the boys were burned beyond recognition. The coffins had to be closed. She never had a chance to see her son, to say goodbye. Later, a driver's education instructor at her son's school told students that the boys "deserved what they got" because they had been drinking and driving. In the midst of the immense pain she already felt, this teacher's comment was especially hurtful.

Marilyn hoped that nothing like this would happen to us, but she simply wanted to warn us that it might. As thoughtful and kind as some people could be, others could be thoughtless and cruel. We needed to be prepared for that. As time went on, Jan and I did not have such painful encounters. The closest we came was a call from the insurance adjuster with regard to Jason's car. He offered us less money than was still owed on the car at the bank and he insisted that we accept his offer, suggesting that it might be even less if we didn't agree to take it right now. Later, the agent from our insurance company called to say they would pay the full amount still owed for the car. He sounded apologetic, perhaps embarrassed. I hope he was.

Much of what Marilyn said turned out to be good advice. She said that Jan and I should be good to ourselves, do things that felt good to us, no matter how crazy they might seem. She said not to do things because we thought other people expected us to do them, but because we needed to do them. She also said that people were going to offer support in various ways and we should accept it. This was important for me to hear, because I have always been more comfortable giving rather than receiving. At Christmas, I have enjoyed watching other people opening presents, but I always felt awkward, even embarrassed, opening the gifts given to me. I don't know why.

Marilyn was offering this advice in the hope that it would help in the grieving process. The process would require confronting and accepting Jason's death. It would take time. Marilyn had spent countless hours thinking about her son's accident, having "conversations" with him where she asked if he now understood why she had always nagged him about being careful and warned him against getting into dangerous situations. She was sitting in bed one morning having such a "conversation" when she was surprised by a reply. She did not hear it, but rather sensed his "response" that she was only saying this because she was still in her physical body. This event was her turning point. This experience allowed her to work through her grief by freeing her emotionally from the grip of despair.

At the end of the conversation Marilyn apologized for calling me. After her son died, she had received phone calls from women she didn't know who had also lost a son or a daughter and at the time she wondered how they could call someone they didn't know to talk about coping with the death of a child, but here she was, making such a call. I told Marilyn not to apologize, that I appreciated what she had to say, that I had been struggling with a multitude of emotions, that I had been mired in confusion, that her words had helped me. It was true. I would think about her advice often in the months ahead.

Later that day another event occurred which offered some comfort. We were listening to the 6 o'clock newscast on the station where Jason had worked as a teleprompter operator for the past two weeks. The anchorman read the following report:

> A La Crosse man is dead tonight following a one car accident late last night. Nineteen year old Jason Koppelman was pronounced dead at a local hospital from injuries he suffered in the crash. The accident happened on County Road 25 in Houston County outside of La Crescent. Witnesses say Koppelman's car left the road and skidded before rolling over several times, throwing him from the vehicle.
>
> To the crew that brings you this newscast, Jason Koppelman's story is especially tragic. Jason was on his way home from TV 19 where last night he worked on this newscast. The entire staff of TV 19 sends its sympathies and prayers to Jason's family and friends.

The word "man" seemed strange to me. This was my child. Jason was not a man, not yet. He had a lot of growing up to do. Or so I had thought; so I had hoped. Yet the article in the newspaper also referred to him as a "man." Jason might have liked this, but he often seemed reluctant to accept the mantle of adulthood. Man or boy, it didn't really matter now, but we took some consolation from the personal expression of sympathy on the newscast. Even drops of water are comforting to those who thirst.

Some comfort came from expected sources. My parents arrived on Friday, the day before the funeral, and stayed for a few days. They were calm. They talked of Jason, of good memories. They talked about family. That was what I needed, to talk about Jason and family and not about work or politics or newspaper headlines. I did not want to think about the world. I wanted conversations where words were cushioned with affection. I didn't need to hear the word "love," but I needed to feel it. That's what my parents gave me. I saw it in their faces and I heard it in their voices. That helped.

Many friends came and did what they could. Jan's brothers searched Jason's car for anything else that might still be in it. Some friends went to Jason's dorm room to collect his clothes, posters, and other possessions. Other friends kept track of the gifts of food and flowers so we would be able to send notes of appreciation later. And so on.

Many tasks could not be delegated to friends because they required decisions only Jan and I could make. This was difficult for me because it was so hard to think. I felt as though my body and mind were deep underwater; I seemed to be moving slowly as though a great weight was pressing down on me. I had to concentrate intensely to perform simple tasks or make simple decisions. The funeral director called to ask if we wanted to put some personal possessions in the coffin with Jason. We didn't know. He also asked Jan to choose some clothes for Jason. What clothes would he have wanted to be buried in? We didn't know. It was not the kind of question you ask your nineteen year old son.

When Keith came to discuss the funeral service. Jan asked him to read a portion of an essay by Garrison Keillor from the book *We Are Still Married* [5]. Jason had often listened to cassette tapes of stories from Keillor's radio program "Prairie Home Companion." When he read Keillor's book, he liked the essay "Laying On Our Backs Looking Up At The Stars" so much that he called some of his friends long distance and read the entire essay to them. He also made several copies of this essay and sent one to Jan and me. Jan gave Keith our copy of the essay because we had not yet found Jason's copy of the book.

Keith asked questions about Jason, about his experiences, his dreams. It was good to talk about him, to remember. I talked about the day Jason was baptized and Keith asked where it was done. As we discussed the event, Keith recognized the name of the minister who had performed the baptismal ceremony. They had met and became good friends at the seminary. One friend to welcome Jason to the world, one to usher him out. It's the sort of thing that makes people say, "small world" and smile. But my world had collapsed and was now so small I felt suffocated in it. There was nothing to smile about.

Keith knew of my love of literature and wondered if I wanted any poetry in the funeral service, but I could not remember Jason liking any particular poem. One of my favorite poems about immortality is the part of *Leaves of Grass* by Walt Whitman which begins, "A child said What is the grass?" [6]. I didn't know if Jason had ever read that poem, so I hesitated to suggest it. Jason had written several poems at college last year, and had shared them with me. I told the minister I would look through Jason's writing to see if I could find something. Later I would find a love poem Jason had written entitled "Encounter." When I showed it to Jan, she agreed that it would be appropriate for the funeral.

Jan tried to find my first wedding band. It had broken in two a few years ago so she had bought me a new one. She wanted to have the original ring repaired so we could put it on Jason's finger. We wanted him to be buried with it. She found it, and I called a local jeweler. At first the woman insisted that it would require three or four days, but when I explained why we needed it right away, she said she would talk to the repairman and call back in thirty minutes. Fifteen minutes later she called back to say that the repairman would have the ring ready for me by Saturday morning if I could bring it to the store right away.

On the way to the jeweler's I stopped at the mortuary to leave my old glasses. Jason's glasses had been lost in the accident and we could not find his spare pair. My old pair would have to do. The visitations were the next ordeal in our torturous journey through the grieving process.

Jason David Koppelman

Koppelman

Jason David Koppelman, 19, of 1017 West Ave. S., died Wednesday, Sept. 13, 1989. He was born in Lincoln, Neb., July 19, 1970, to Kent and Janet (Gross) Koppelman. He was a 1988 graduate of Central High School and was a sophomore at Viterbo College, intending to pursue a career in film and broadcasting. He was employed at WXOW where he operated a teleprompter.

He is survived by his parents of La Crosse; a sister, Tess at home; his maternal grandfather, Harold Gross of Omaha, Neb.; and his paternal grandparents, Roy and Lois Koppelman of Winnetoon, Neb. He was preceded in death by his maternal grandmother.

Services will be held Saturday, Sept. 16, at 2 p.m. in Sletten McKee Hanson Funeral Home. The Rev. Keith Kensinger will officiate, and burial will be in Oak Grove Cemetery. Friends may call at the funeral home today from 6 to 8 p.m. Memorials may be given to La Crosse Foundation Scholarship Fund.

Reprinted with permission from *La CrosseTribune*, September 14, 1989, La Crosse, Wisconsin.

Remembering the child . . .

Talking to Keith about Jason's baptism brought back memories of his birth and childhood. I recalled the day I was to pick up Jan and this baby boy, our first child, from the hospital. I had traded in our old car, a badly battered Mercury, so I could arrive at the hospital to greet my wife and son behind the wheel of a brand new (1970) Datsun stationwagon. I was under the illusion that I could afford a new car because I had just signed a teaching contract. I had a job! I wanted to do something to symbolize the beginning of a new life for all three of us, but for Jason in particular. When I drove into the hospital driveway, Jan didn't see me because she was looking for the old Mercury. When she finally recognized me behind the wheel of this bright red car, the look of surprise quickly dissolved into a smile. And I could hardly contain my joy.

Jason was a good baby. He rarely cried; he was seldom sick. He made parenting seem easy. I especially appreciated this after Tess was born. Tess introduced us to a different set of parenting experiences. Fortunately for me she was born six years later when I was better prepared to deal with a more challenging child.

Jason demonstrated some special qualities early in his childhood, like his ability to entertain himself. During my first years of teaching, I might come home from school feeling exhausted and simply collapse on the couch as soon as I walked in the door. Often Jason would come to me and want to play, but I would simply say, "Daddy doesn't feel like playing right now and he needs to rest for a little while. OK?" Jason would say "OK" and he would go off and play by himself for thirty or forty minutes or more. Parenting certainly didn't seem so difficult. When Tess was that age, she would also respond to such a request by saying "OK," but in thirty or forty *seconds* she would be back wanting to play. From talking to other parents, Tess's behavior was more "typical."

If there was a problem with this ability to be alone, it was that Jason could be so content playing by himself that he was often not interested in playing with other children. He would sometimes resist efforts to get him to play with other children. Given a choice, Jason would rather be with his parents, who were obviously his preferred playmates. It worried me. This continued through elementary school and even into his middle school years. We moved twice during this time which probably contributed to his preference, especially since Jason did not make friends easily.

Being your child's "best friend" can be difficult for active adults involved in careers, but Jason didn't mind. He would wait patiently until either mom or dad had time to play with him. In retrospect, I am glad that we spent so much time with each other. It is still difficult to believe that I will never see him, that we will never talk or touch, that we will never be together.

As a toddler Jason always wanted to be under or inside something. In family albums, there are pictures of this cherubic little boy with long auburn hair (curled up at the end) standing under the kitchen table, sitting under a chair, crawling under a coffee table at his grandparents' house. He loved being in boxes, in his play pen, in any confined area. Perhaps it made him feel safe.

This desire for safety was certainly apparent when Jason was learning to walk. Like most children, he first started to walk by holding on to someone's hand or to furniture, but he required such support well past the time when it was necessary. He had obviously developed the strength and balance to walk without help, but he still wanted a couch or chair or table for support. The moment he had nothing left to hold onto, he would drop down to his knees and crawl.

During that summer Jan and I were taking graduate classes at the University of Nebraska. We rented a house owned by an elderly woman who had fallen and broken her hip. Her family wanted someone to stay in the house for a few months while she recuperated. The house had many more tables and chairs than we had in our sparsely furnished apartment, so Jason had more furniture to hold onto and was walking more than ever.

On the morning of the fourth of July, two weeks before Jason's first birthday, Jan and I were preparing for a party for a few friends. I was in the living room and Jason was standing on the other side of the room gripping a chair seat. Suddenly he let go of the chair and started walking toward "daddy." After a moment of surprise, I shouted at Jan to "come quick!" My shout startled Jason and he stopped walking, but he did not drop to his knees. He was still standing in the middle of the living room when Jan came in.

I told Jason to come and beckoned to him. I don't know if this restored his confidence or reminded him of his original intent, but he continued walking over to me and I gave him a big hug. Jan began to praise him so I said, "Go see Mom." Jason took off unassisted and walked right over to her, receiving more hugs and kisses. He walked by himself for the rest of the day. It was as if he didn't think he could walk by himself but did it without thinking, proving to himself that he could. It was a memorable Fourth of July, a kind of "Independence Day" for Jason, too.

Such memories of Jason's childhood provided a desired distraction, but they were only a temporary respite from reality. We are often told to remember the past in order to understand the present, but sometimes to remember the past is to forget the present. I needed sporadic moments of forgetfulness.

We moved to Connecticut when Jason was three years old. I had accepted a position as a teacher and Assistant Headmaster at a private school in Bridgeport and we lived in a large apartment attached to the school. The school was in an older part of town with many lovely old homes although many had been converted to apartments and showed signs of deterioration. We rarely saw any neighbors and Jason's only contact with other children was at pre-school. Although Tuller School was run by nuns, it was no longer a Catholic school. The children were from a variety of religious, racial and ethnic backgrounds.

Jason was taken to school each morning in a long white station wagon. By the time it came for him there were a number of children already in it. He was home by midafternoon. Jason's teacher was "Miss Margaret." She played the piano, and sang, and taught the children letters and numbers. Jason adored her. The Headmistress was Sister Vera who would occasionally visit the pre-school classroom at which time the children would stand and greet her by chanting "Good morning Sister Beer-ah." Jason was mystified by her. He had never seen a nun before.

Jason loved going to pre-school, partly because of the activities, the singing, the games, but primarily because of the kids. He was beginning to develop a little interest in playing with other children, and it was at Tuller School that he met and became friends with a black girl. Jason often talked about Deena. During the fall and winter I hadn't seen any children in the neighborhood, so I didn't realize until early spring that Deena lived only two blocks away, and that the white station wagon stopped at her house right after ours. Now Jason and Deena began to spend their Saturdays together as well, riding their Big Wheels up and down the sidewalk, playing on his swing set, or spreading an array of toys across the living room floor.

One Saturday when Deena was at our house she asked to use the bathroom. Jason decided he needed to use the bathroom, too, so Jan helped them both with their snaps and zippers and Jason went off with Deena. In a few minutes Jason ran back to Jan with a look of astonishment saying, "Mom! Mom! Deena's black all over!" It had never dawned on him that it wasn't just her face and hands that were dark. I sometimes wondered if Deena was surprised that Jason was "white all over." Deena was the first in a long line of female friends, and Tuller was Jason's first school. Both set the standards for Jason's expectations of playmates and school.

When summer came we found ourselves moving once again, this time to Iowa. We bought a white ranch-style house near the edge of town. The house had a large yard, a giant sandbox (used as a litter box by neighborhood cats), and a prodigious apple tree with an abundance of low limbs suitable for climbing. On the day we moved in, I observed a number of dirt smudged tow-headed boys ranging from two to seven years old playing in the yard across the street. Perhaps Jason would find new friends right away. I later discovered that the Lackey family lived in that house. For Jason they would become *The Lackey Boys*, and they primarily served to reinforce his continuing preference for female playmates.

The Lackey Boys lived in the house catty-corner from us. To this day I can't say exactly how many there were, perhaps a half a dozen (their numbers would swell during the summer when they were visited by relatives from nearby farms). All of the children had the same dirty faces, runny noses, sun-bleached blonde hair, and dusty bare feet (or raggedy sneakers with frayed gray shoestrings flapping untied). From early spring until late fall they swarmed across the neighborhood in shorts slung low exposing rounded brown bellies beneath the multi-colored striped T-shirts you find in packages of three at rural discount stores (which always shrink after one washing so they come down to an inch above the belly button). The boys weren't bad. They were just a little wild. They liked to roughhouse, roll around in the dirt, push and shove each other and punch their friends in the shoulder. Jason hated them one and all.

Fortunately Jason had an alternative. Trisha lived directly across the street from us. She was a year older than Jason and she soon became his "first love." They spent nearly every day together. Whether they played in the yard or in the house, they were careful to stay out of sight of *The Lackey Boys*. Trisha introduced Jason to her friends, and he was soon surrounded with a veritable harem. When we celebrated his fifth birthday the next summer, Jason had about ten friends at his party— all girls.

Jason and Trisha did everything together that first summer. One time they put on a show in our back yard. They unhooked the swings from the swing set and draped old blankets over the crossbar to make a stage. They sang and danced to records and put on a play using puppets and dolls. Everything was fine until they invited Trisha's friends to the performance, and for some reason they included *The Lackey Boys*. That was a mistake. The boys were not impressed with the show, and the older ones simply drifted off after a few minutes. The youngest boys stayed, but they were not content to sit passively in the audience; they wanted to be in the show. They jumped up from where they sat in the grass and tried to come on stage. Jason tried to fend them off, but to no avail. The show ended when *The Lackey Boys* brought the curtain down. Literally. Jason and Trisha were beside themselves with rage.

That fall Trisha started kindergarten, and Jason, being a year younger, was stuck at home. He missed going to school. Like most small towns, there was no nursery school or day care. If a mother had a job, she relied on friends, neighbors, and especially relatives for her child care. Children from area farms attended kindergarten in the morning and children in town attended in the afternoon. At noon each day Jason would sit at our living room window and watch Trisha walk down the street to the corner where she met her friends. For the first few weeks Jason sulked. Jan tried to occupy him with puzzles and games and other activities; she took him to the park a few times, but that didn't help. The park was across the street from the school playground, so going there was like rubbing salt in the wound.

Trisha would come home from school each day and tell Jason about everything she had done. Jason, of course, knew about school and what went on there, so he was not impressed by her descriptions. It only made him miss Tuller School. When they played "school," Trisha now insisted on being the teacher, since she saw herself as the authority on what went on in school. Jason was relegated to the role of her student. He didn't care for the part.

One Saturday morning Jason had been playing at Trisha's house when he suddenly came stomping across the street. He marched into the house slamming the door behind him. He charged into the kitchen, pulled out bread, peanut butter and jelly, and slapped together a sandwich. He stuffed the sandwich into a plastic bag, grabbed a handful of cookies and rifled through the cupboard until he found the Flintstones lunchbox he had used at Tuller School. He slopped milk all over the kitchen table trying to fill the thermos and then he threw thermos, sandwich, and cookies into the lunch box and slammed the lid shut. Jan and I watched all of this, not really certain how to intervene. Jason was so angry and so serious. Finally, he gathered up his lunch box, grabbed a fist full of pencils and the small notebook we kept by the phone, and stomped toward the door.

"Wait a minute, Mister!" Jan called out, "Where do you think you're going?" He turned and looked her square in the eye. He had his jaw pushed out and his teeth were clenched. It was the fiercest expression I had ever seen on his face.

"I'm going to school!" After this emphatic declaration, he whirled around dramatically, flung the door open and walked out.

Jan went after him, but he was moving fast. By the time she caught up with him he was near the end of the block. His jaw was set and his teeth were still clenched, but she also saw the big tears running down his bright red face. She put her arm around him and tried to calm him down. Through the convulsing sobs he said he knew he could not just suddenly go to school, but he was trying to "show Trisha." Mother and son walked silently back home, taking the alley behind our house so Trisha wouldn't see them returning.

The next fall Jason started kindergarten, but this school didn't seem to be as much fun as he remembered. The children sat in assigned seats in rows and spent much of their time working in workbooks. There was not much time for games, activities, or music. I asked Jason how he liked school after his first day and he only said that there wasn't a piano in his classroom. It was not like Tuller School. Nothing would ever match that experience.

Jan was happy that she was able to stay home for a couple of years with Jason before he started school. When I had taken my first teaching job in a small town in Nebraska, Jan found a job teaching in a town nearby. This was especially fortunate because I had not realistically calculated the take home pay for a first year teacher when I purchased the new car. It would have been difficult to make the payments on one salary, but now our problem was that we only had a couple of weeks to find a babysitter for Jason. We were told to talk to a woman named Rita. She had raised ten children and her youngest child was now in junior high school. It had been a long time since there had been a baby in her home, and Jason was only six weeks old when we first brought him to her. He became her eleventh baby.

Rita was incredibly wise in the ways of children. Whenever Jason was sick or just "fussy," we always called Rita first and followed her advice before taking him to the doctor. We were fortunate to have found her because we learned so much from her. After two years we moved, but we always tried to stop at Rita's whenever we returned to Nebraska.

During one such visit, I was talking about Jason being such a gentle, affectionate boy and Rita said he was always affectionate, even as a baby. I asked how she could tell. Whenever her babies would wake up from a nap, Rita would lean over the crib and put her face close to the baby's face. The babies would have different reactions. Some of her babies would just lie there passively and look at her, others would reach up and try to push her face away with their hands. Jason always raised his hand to her face and stroked her cheek.

I had always appreciated this part of Jason's personality, but I also knew that our society does not reward boys for having this quality. In fact, such boys will usually "pay a price." A gentle, affectionate boy runs the risk of being harassed by other boys intent on proving themselves— their "toughness," their masculinity. Some boys never stop doing this, even as men. Jason had many unpleasant experiences throughout his life because of boys who engage in such behavior. I think it confused him more than it hurt him. But it did hurt.

When we moved to Wisconsin, Jason attended an elementary school where these abusive encounters became more frequent. The number of incidents seemed to increase as the boys discovered that Jason didn't like to fight. He tried unsuccessfully to avoid them. When school started the next year Jason thought he would have an easier time because he would be in fifth grade, the highest grade level at the school. The fifth grade boys who had picked on him last year were in middle school now, and his classmates never bothered him. Unfortunately, some fourth grade boys started being verbally abusive, which ultimately lead to some pushing and shoving.

Jason hated it. He didn't even like talking about it, but we did talk. I suggested different ways to react to the boys, but the options were limited. Jason knew that Jan and I didn't approve of fighting, and fighting did not appeal to him either. I reluctantly admitted that fighting back might be the only way to make the fourth grade boys stop. I was glad that Jason did not want to fight and I told him so. I hoped he could find a non-violent solution, but I had to be honest and admit that it might not be possible to avoid fighting.

Finally, one particular fourth grade boy who had been a persistent antagonist confronted Jason during recess. He started calling Jason names and then pushed Jason hard, trying to knock him down. Suddenly, Jason punched the boy in the stomach as hard as he could. The boy crumpled to his knees, tears in his eyes, gasping for breath. After that incident, the fourth grade boys left Jason alone. They would still call him names or threaten him, but they kept their distance. That was all right with Jason. He could tolerate their verbal attacks as long as they didn't physically attack him.

Jason talked about punching the boy during supper. He seemed almost surprised at how easy it was, at how fast the boy went down. He almost seemed to be gloating, but I don't think he was. To take pleasure from inflicting pain on someone was not characteristic of Jason, but I think he felt victorious. He had defeated his tormentor; he had overcome evil. It may have been experiences like this that later made him such a fan of the "Star Wars" movies.

Punching that boy was probably something Jason had to do. I was glad that it resulted in the other boys leaving him alone, but it still makes me angry that boys are not permitted to be gentle. Jason lost some of his gentleness that day, and some of his innocence. This experience did not "make a man" of him, nor did it make him a better person. He lost far more than he gained. I have always found it difficult to determine if our society actually believes in the value of such hostile and hurtful behavior or if we are merely stupid in our apparent willingness to perpetuate this particular perception of "masculinity."

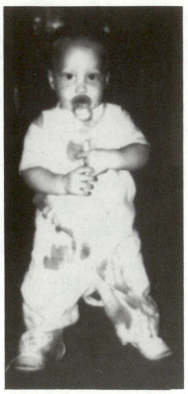

CHAPTER 3
The Necessary Ordeal

. . . there is
special providence in the fall of a sparrow.
If it be now, 'tis not to come; if it be not
to come, it will be now; if it be not now,
yet it will come — the readiness is all. [7, p. 971]

William Shakespeare
Hamlet Act 5, Scene 2

The private visitation for family was scheduled for Friday afternoon. The mortuary was only a few blocks from our house, so my parents walked. It was a beautiful September day, but I didn't want to walk. It would be too exhausting. I still felt as though I was walking underwater, moving in slow motion. It was a struggle to keep going, resisting the temptation to simply stop, to give up. I was aware of my heart beating, of my lungs breathing. It was as though I had to direct those activities consciously, as though a part of my brain had been damaged.

When I walked into the visitation room at the mortuary, I saw the coffin. It seemed huge and heavy and dark in contrast to the flowers on either side of it, bouquets of flowers so delicate and graceful, such bright colors. I was surprised by the flowers. I had not thought about people sending flowers, and there were so many.

I walked up to the coffin. Jason looked uncomfortable, as though he was squeezed a little tight around the shoulders. He had wide shoulders. His face (so still, so strange) resembled its appearance in life. I have been to funerals where the face in the coffin looked like a wax statue based on a bad photograph. Since Jason's head injuries had been extensive, I knew he must have lost portions of his scalp, but his hair was arranged to conceal this. His hair was parted opposite the side he normally parted it to cover a crescent shaped cut, barely visible on the edge of his hairline. The shape of the cut suggested that he may have hit his head on the steering wheel. He would have looked better if we could have found his spare pair of glasses rather than using my old pair, but the face belonged to Jason. The stillness belonged to death. (Where was life? Does it disappear at death's coming, fleeing like a shadow at the stroke of noon?) The mortician had done a good job. Everyone said so. I thanked the mortician for his efforts.

The funeral director asked if I wanted the coffin closed at the public visitation that evening. There were so many cracks in the back of the skull that the embalming fluid was leaking. He had a towel under Jason's head at the moment, but he recommended closing the coffin during the public visitation. I discussed his suggestion with Jan, but we both wanted an open coffin. When I have gone to funerals it has been important for me to see the body in order to accept the reality of that person's death. It is even more important when the person who died was young. It is a necessary ordeal in the grieving process. There are no short cuts.

At the family visitation, Jan and I were touching Jason's hands, stroking his cheek. The nurse had warned us about the possibility of swelling around the eyes after they had been removed, but this had not happened. The main difference between the body now compared to the hospital became apparent when I touched his arms and chest. They felt so heavy, as though filled with sand. It was helpful to touch the body at the hospital because it felt a little like touching Jason when he was alive. The difference then was the lack of warmth, the lack of response, the stillness. Touching him now was like touching something else, a non-Jason that looked like Jason. But still we touched him. We kissed him. Trying to find the words to say goodbye.

The two hours passed so quickly. When we were not looking at the body, Jan and I talked quietly with the others. More bouquets were brought in. We looked at the flowers; we read the cards; we wept. Some of the flowers came from surprising sources. There was a large bouquet of roses from the men who worked at the gas station near our house, and another bouquet from the secondary education staff at Iowa State University where I had received my doctorate ten years ago. I wondered how they had heard of Jason's death so quickly. There were flowers from the Taco John's where Jason had worked during high school and two bouquets from the television station where Jason had just started to work. Many flowers were from family and friends, some from those too far away to attend the funeral.

In the past I had questioned the practice of sending flowers to funerals. Yes, they were beautiful, but what purpose did they serve? To remind us of the brevity of life? Would that be a comforting thought at such a moment? I preferred to send money to the family for whatever memorial or charity they chose, but now I realized how much I appreciated the flowers. Amid the tumult of my despair they spoke gently. Although they did suggest "how fragile is life," they also said "and how precious," perhaps more precious because of that fragility. The flowers reminded me of the affection of friends, of the bonds of family, of love. They comforted me. I was grateful to those who had sent them and often found tears in my eyes as I read the cards.

The two hours passed so quickly. We had to leave. It was time for everyone to get some rest and some food since we would soon be returning for the public visitation. Jan and I went back to the coffin again, looked at Jason again, touched him again, kissed him again. I kissed him on the cheek and stepped back. Jan leaned over and kissed him on the lips. I experienced an emotional chaos (agony-pity-rage-despair-love-helplessness) which was almost overwhelming as I watched her kiss those lifeless lips.

Thinking about Jason's death was especially difficult because I did not question why this was happening to me. Such a question may provide some people with a distraction from their grief, and perhaps offered a way to accept a loved one's death, but I have long understood that no one is exempt from suffering, that "bad things happen to good people." I can understand why someone might want to believe that you get what you deserve in life. If you have a comfortable life, it is pleasant to believe this is so because you have worked hard and deserve to be comfortable, but such a belief also suggests that if someone is suffering then they have done something wrong and are getting what they deserve. Such a belief estranges the believer from those who suffer, and each of us will suffer, sometime. This estrangement is the hideous face behind the smiling mask of that seemingly benign belief.

Instead of such conjecture I was left with the simple but indisputable thought that I had not had to face a tragedy in my life while other people had endured them. I could not ask "Why me?" without asking "Why anyone?" If I tried to think of a possible purpose in Jason's death, I would invariably be forced to recognize that senseless things happened to people all the time. Any attempt to make sense of this tragedy would be inadequate because any meaning would be of my own invention. The inescapable conclusion was that bad things happened to people, and now something bad had happened to me. It was my turn to suffer. That was the simple truth, but there was no comfort in it.

The announcement in the newspaper stated that the hours for the public visitation were from 6:00 to 8:00 on Friday evening. We hoped we would not have to stay longer. When we returned to the mortuary a little before six o'clock, Matt was there setting up his "boom box." He had recorded a variety of Jason's favorite movie themes as we had asked. Jan and Tess and I went up to the coffin to look at Jason and to touch him once again. The movie themes played quietly as people began to come in. I stood near the open portion of the coffin with Jan and Tess on my right. This allowed people to see Jason first before speaking to us. As time passed, I kept moving closer to Jason, often ending up in front of the coffin so that I was blocking people's view of him. Several times Jan tugged at my arm to pull me back, away from the coffin.

The first person to arrive was a former student of mine who had also been one of Jason's teachers. Later on Jan and I would be introduced to a despondent young man with a thin, black mustache who seemed unable to look at us. He was introduced as one of Jason's co-workers at the television station, the one the paramedics mentioned who had been driving behind Jason the night of the accident and had stopped to help. I shook his hand and said I appreciated everything he had done. He seemed so sad that I thanked him again for trying to save my son. By 6:30 a line of people had developed, and as time passed it got longer:

> people I knew—people I didn't know—people who worked with me—people who worked with Jan—people who worked with Jason—neighbors—friends of Tess—friends of Jason—a young man in a marching band uniform—Jason on everyone's lips—sadness in everyone's voice—muffled sounds of grief—words of comfort—words in response—a blur of sound and sight—handshakes from some—hugs from others—gestures of love—looks of concern—sorrow you could hear—sorrow you could feel—tears from them—tears from me—so many tears my eyes dried up and I could not cry

As the end of the line finally approached, Jan slumped down in exhaustion on a folding chair behind her. She had been calm and strong throughout the visitation. She had shed few tears, but now they poured forth as though furious at having been restrained for so long. My mother sat down and put her arm around Jan and spoke softly. It was 8:00. We could go home.

Most of the family had arrived and they gathered at our house with a few of our friends. Many people had brought food to the house in a variety of plastic containers which covered the kitchen counter. In the living room, Tess was playing a videotape of some old home movies. Since we had bought the camera shortly after Tess was born, many of the scenes focussed on her, but Jason was there. He was seven and eight years old then, dancing and laughing and playing ball and mugging for the camera. Seeing the videotape was not like remembering, and I could not bear to watch it. That little boy on the videotape was clearly exuberant and alive, but my boy was dead. I was not even sure I could connect the two.

After an hour people began to leave. It was getting late, they said, we'll see you tomorrow. Tomorrow. At the funeral. At last everyone left except my parents who were staying with us. They said they were tired, and bid us goodnight. Although desperately tired, I was not sure I would be able to sleep. Besides, Jan and I needed some time together, just to talk, not about anything in particular, just to be together. It was almost midnight when we walked upstairs.

5:00 a.m. — I was awake once again.

I seemed to have a mental alarm clock set to wake me at this time. For the second morning in a row I got out of bed, knowing that I had not had enough sleep, not knowing what else to do. I went to the bathroom and came back to bed. I hoped I would go back to sleep, but I was wide awake. My mind was a whirlwind of thoughts about Jason, about the accident, about the visitation last night.

One woman's comment had distressed me. After expressing her sympathy, she said her daughter had almost accepted a job at the same television station where Jason worked. Her daughter didn't take the job because she didn't want to be driving in the winter on that winding road to the top of the bluff. I wondered how dangerous that road was. Should I have driven on it before Jason started working at the station? I had talked to Jason about the road but he didn't say it was dangerous. He only said it might be difficult to drive during the winter. I had suggested that he use Jan's car on such days since it had four wheel drive. Now I wanted to drive on that road. I wanted to see the site of the accident. I wanted to see where my son died.

As I lay in bed, unable to sleep, I thought of my recent sense of reconciliation with death. Jason had not had the chance to enjoy life as I had, nor to have such thoughts of reconciliation. He was preparing to live, not to die. When Jan's mother died a few years ago, Jason would hardly look at her during the family visitation. While Tess and Jan and

I stood by the coffin saying goodbye, Jason walked along the walls of the room as if to keep as much distance between himself and the coffin as possible. He loved his grandmother, but he was clearly uncomfortable with the idea of her death. And now he was dead. Now he was the one in the coffin with no choice about being there. My stomach was churning. I got up and went to the bathroom. The emotional turmoil had affected my bowels the past two days, and would continue to do so for several more.

When I came back to bed, Jan was dressing. It was 7:00. Jan went downstairs and I thought I should join her and help prepare breakfast. My parents would probably get up soon. I kept thinking about Jason and how unprepared he was to die. The thought distressed me, haunted me. In the midst of this agonizing the words "Ask, and it shall be given you; seek, and ye shall find; knock, and it shall be opened unto you" kept forming in my mind. It was not like a voice, but the words insistently entered my consciousness. I finally folded my hands to pray. I had not prayed in years. I had not had anything to say nor anything to ask. I had simply wanted to live my life as best as I could and God, if God existed, could decide what to do with me when I died.

I began to pray, still besieged by doubts, but feeling lost in a fog of pain, urged on by a need I could not ignore. In my prayer I whispered my doubts to God and apologized for them, but I felt I had to be truthful and the truth was that even as I prayed I was doubting, questioning whether there was a God to hear me. I spoke of my anguish about Jason's death, about how unprepared he was to die and how that worried me. Tears welled up. I believed that something survived the death of the body even though I did not know what it was or how it happened. I said I was not praying for myself, for an assurance of my immortality, because I had begun my own process of becoming reconciled with death (as an omniscient God would surely know). What I needed was for God, if God existed, to give me some kind of assurance about Jason.

Part of being a parent is doing things to help prepare your child for a new experience or to suggest solutions to a problem. Now there was nothing I could do. This was one of the burdens weighing on me. I asked for a sign of some kind to let me know that Jason was all right, to show me that I need not worry. That was all I wanted from God. It seemed a small favor to ask in exchange for the anguish I must bear for the rest of my life. I tried to keep bitterness out of my voice as I finished the prayer. I am not certain I succeeded.

Later that morning, I went to the jewelry store to pick up my wedding ring. It had been repaired so well you could not tell where it had been broken. Jan was pleased, and she was also pleased that she finally found Jason's spare pair of glasses under some papers in a desk drawer. We talked briefly about the funeral. On an impulse I said I wanted the minister to read one of my favorite excerpts from *Leaves of Grass* [6]. She told me to call him. First I wanted to find my copy of the book, but it wasn't among my poetry books. I couldn't find it anywhere. When I called Keith, he agreed to read the excerpt but he couldn't find his copy either. Some friends offered to go downtown and buy a copy. They stopped at the closest bookstore and asked for the book. At first the clerk said she could not find it, but they noticed that she was looking among the gardening books. They found one copy in the poetry section and bought it.

Around noon the phone rang and the caller asked if someone would be at the house during the funeral. I said we had arranged to have someone here. The caller said he would drop off some food at that time and abruptly hung up. I thought it was odd that the caller never identified himself nor offered any condolences. We had been told to have someone at the house during the visitations and the funeral because thieves have taken advantage of such occasions to break into homes. Such is the world we live in.

It was time to leave. Jan and I needed to be at the mortuary early to replace my old glasses with Jason's spare pair. We also had decided on some items to place in the coffin: my wedding ring, a book on film-making which Jason had generously highlighted with a yellow magic marker, a picture of the family taken last Christmas, and a farewell letter written by one of his friends. This letter was from a girl who had worked with Jason and who shared his interest in poetry. Leaving the house, we were greeted by another warm, beautiful autumn day, a gentle breeze occasionally stirring the multicolored leaves.

When Jan and I walked into the mortuary, Matt was already there with two photographs he wanted to put in the coffin. One picture showed Matt in dark glasses with an arm around his basset hound, Bart, also wearing dark glasses. The other picture was of the group of students who had gone on a school trip to Washington D.C. during Jason's senior year. Jason had a great time on that trip, and some friendships grew out of it. Matt also had a copy of the "Bloom County" comic strip which featured Opus, a penguin with a big beak, big feet and a big bottom. Matt had brought the final strip which showed Opus walking into the sunset, battered suitcase in hand.

"Bloom County" was Jason's favorite comic strip. He had three stuffed Opus dolls.

Keith was there and said he had found his copy of *Leaves of Grass* so Jan put the copy our friends had bought in the coffin. Jan arranged everything in the coffin (wedding ring on Jason's little finger, books by his side, pictures and letters in his hands), then we went to the area designated for the family. The funeral director came over and pointed out the door leading to the parking lot outside. After the funeral, family members would go out that door and the cars belonging to family and friends would be lined up behind the hearse.

The area for family members was off to the side of the main area where the rest of the people sat facing the coffin. We watched as people came in. Those who had been unable to come to the public visitation went up to the front to see Jason; others came in and immediately sat down; others came over to us to express their sympathy. The funeral director asked if Jan and Tess and I wanted to look at Jason one last time. We walked over to the coffin. Tess gave Jason's body a little hug and Jan leaned over and kissed his cheek, but I only watched. I felt so tired, so numb. I knew it would not help me to touch that cold flesh again. What I needed was to touch a living person. I put my arms around Jan and Tess as we walked back to our chairs. After we sat down, the folding doors were extended in front of us to block our view while the coffin was closed; then the folding doors were pushed back. This was the signal for the funeral to start.

You could barely hear the anonymous organist playing "In the Garden." Jason would have hated this taped music. I was distracted from the music for a moment by a scraping sound coming from the door to the parking lot. The door seemed to have moved an inch or two, as if someone outside had turned the door knob and tried to pull the door open but the door was stuck and only moved slightly. I wondered if it was the wind. I thought about walking over to the door and pulling it shut so it wouldn't blow open. Suddenly, the door flew open, banging loudly on the outside wall as if a child had barrelled through in a hurry to get outside on such a warm autumn day. Jan's brother walked over and closed the door.

I thought of the sign I had asked for in my prayer that morning, but then rejected such a supernatural explanation. It must have been the wind; it was a coincidence; it meant nothing. Then I thought, "What do you want? Is God supposed to appear before your eyes beamed down from the transporter room in 'Star Trek'? Did you expect something like the movie version of Moses parting the Red Sea? You asked for a

sign and you got it. You can take it or leave it, but that's all you get."
Part of me wanted to believe that Jason's spirit had just gone out that
door, that this was the "sign" for which I had prayed. Part of me still
doubted.

When the taped music mercifully concluded, Keith read from the
Bible, followed by a eulogy written by Chuck Sween, one of the
pallbearers, and read by one of Jason's favorite teachers. Chuck was
the first friend Jason made after we had moved to Wisconsin. I remembered the first time I saw him with his red hair (redder than Jason's)
and his shy smile, I liked him right away. As an adolescent he did not
become arrogant or rebellious but was always kind and caring to his
parents and his friends. He was easy to be with, and Jason appreciated
that. I found it easy to talk to him as well, and I liked his willingness to
discuss serious issues. So I listened carefully to his eulogy, and his
words prompted a variety of thoughts.

> When one of your best friends dies at such an early age, you can't
> help but think—"What would his life have been like?" or "Would he
> have been successful?"

Like most parents, I had often thought about Jason's future. Jan and I
had several discussions about supporting his plans (or his fantasy) of
pursuing a career in film. We encouraged him to develop an alternative
plan, just in case. We didn't want to discourage him but we didn't want
him to be disappointed if he was not able to find his niche in the film
industry, and especially if he was not able to achieve his ultimate goal
of directing films.

> . . . because Jason always seemed to know what he wanted out
> of life.

That was true, but I worried that life might not give him an opportunity to get what he wanted. Now it was no longer a question. Death
had given the answer.

> He always set goals for himself, and he always seemed to manage
> somehow or other to achieve his goals. That was one of the things I
> loved about him the most!

I liked this, even though Jason's goals were often based on wonderful
but impractical dreams. I had hoped for other goals. I wanted him to

challenge himself, intellectually, or musically or even athletically, but Jason just wanted to enjoy himself. Although he loved music, Jason hated the stress of music contests. He hated to perform if he was being evaluated. He wanted to play for himself, for the fun of it. I watched him play a solo on the marimba during his senior year. His face was flushed and his lips were tightly clamped. Afterwards he would hardly talk to me even though I tried to compliment him on his performance.

> Jason seemed to know that he had the brains to do what he wanted to do. He was a very good student. He always took the challenging courses and the accelerated ones. It was as if he had a timetable for his plan. Maybe he did.

I had to smile at the claim that Jason was a "good student." He did well in those subjects that interested him, but not in others. If he did not like a course he would forget to complete the homework or he would forget to hand it in, and his grades suffered. He took accelerated classes, but not always willingly. When he registered for his first semester at Iowa, I had to persuade him to take advantage of an opportunity to enroll in their accelerated program.

> He always wanted to go to college, and of course, his major was to be film. He was always interested in films, books, music, and any other thing that allowed him to show his most wonderful talent of all—his ability to think imaginatively and creatively. He was always coming up with new ideas for assignments, songs, books, and his favorite of all, movies! Jason was a connoisseur of movies . . .

As strong as that last statement was, it was still an understatement. If Jason saw a movie only once, it was obviously a terrible film. He would see a mediocre film two or three times. If a film was excellent he would see it in the theatre as often as his finances allowed and when it came out on videotape he would rent it several times.

> When I got the phone call Thursday morning at 1:00 from my friend Matt telling me that our good friend Jason was dead, I was shocked. I must have cried for over an hour.

How hard it must be for a young person to experience the death of a friend. It is difficult enough for an adult. To be nineteen is to be at the beginning. It does not seem possible for life to end at nineteen. When you are young it does not seem possible that a slip of the foot, a little carelessness could end it all. It is a discomforting thought; of course, truth is seldom "comfortable."

> I have always imagined him being very successful in the movie industry . . . This is what I find hard to believe—that I will never be able to go to the theater and see one of his films.

Jason liked to think big. He dreamed of directing a film before he was thirty. He could be very convincing. He apparently convinced his friends. I had always thought of Jason's plans for a film career as a fantasy, but I know how important it is to have dreams, whether they come true or not. It was good to hear this description of how passionately Jason had believed in his dream. What Chuck had written was like a love letter. Friends don't often write love letters. Jason would have appreciated this one.

Keith stepped forward now and announced that he was going to read an excerpt from an essay by Garrison Keillor which Jason liked. He began to read, ". . . And then we lay down on our backs and looked up at the sky full of stars. . ."

> The sky was clear. Lying there, looking up at 180 degrees of billions of dazzling single brilliances, made us feel we had gone away and left the farm far behind.
>
> As we usually see the sky, it is a backdrop, the sky over our house, the sky beyond the clotheslines, but lying down eliminates the horizon and rids us of that strange realistic perspective of the sky as a canopy centered over our heads, and we see the sky as what it is: everything known and unknown, the universe, the whole beach other than the grain of sand we live on . . . Looking out there, my son lying on my chest, I could imagine my grandchildren, and they were more real to me than Congress.
>
> I imagined them strong and free, curious, sensual, indelibly cheerful and affectionate, open-handed—sympathetic to pain and misery and quick in charity, proud when insulted and modest if praised, fiercely loyal to friends, loving God and the beautiful world including our land, from the California coast to the North Dakota prairie to faraway Manhattan, loving music and our American language—when you look at the stars you don't think small. [5, pp. 215-216]

Several days after the service, a friend asked why we had included Keillor's essay in the funeral. I suppose it did seem odd, with its talk of stars and grandchildren, but Jason liked it. That meant he was in it somehow, or it was in him. That prose spoke of Jason in a way that nothing else could, and its conclusion contained perhaps a hint of what Jason may have thought about the possibility of immortality:

> A fly flew in my mouth and went deep, forcing me to swallow, inducing a major life change for him, from fly to simple protein, and so shall we all be changed someday, but here under heaven our spirits are immense, we are so blessed. The stars in the sky, my friends in the grass, my son asleep on my chest, his hands clutching my shirt. [5, p. 216]

Jason had told me he liked to imagine himself as the young child lying on my chest. I liked the image. I will keep it close to me, always.

After the Keillor essay, Keith read Jason's poem entitled "Encounter." It was as good a representation of Jason's personality as I could find:

> What is love
> but that which entrances our minds
> and our hearts
> into believing that what is before us
> is real rather than fantasy.
>
> It is this primary emotion
> that drives us to delve deeper
> into what sparks our imaginations.
> It expands an instant into experience
> to create an entirely new range of
> feeling.
>
> What is love?
>
> It is that initial fascination with beauty
> and the encounter of life that results.

Jason's poem was followed by more taped music from the anonymous organist accompanied now by an equally anonymous voice singing "Amazing Grace." Once again I disliked the music and was certain that Jason would have hated it. The song was fine, but I should have asked someone to sing it. I was upset that I had not thought of this—too many details, too many decisions. At the conclusion of the song, Keith read Walt Whitman:

A child said What is the grass? fetching it to me with full hands;
How could I answer the child? I do not know what it is any more
than he.

I guess it must be the flag of my disposition, out of hopeful green
stuff woven.

Or I guess it is the handkerchief of the Lord,
A scented gift and remembrancer designedly dropt,
Bearing the owner's name someway in the corners, that we may see
and remark and say Whose?

Or I guess the grass is itself a child, the produced babe of the
vegetation.

Or I guess it is a uniform hieroglyphic,
And it means, Sprouting alike in broad zones and narrow zones,
Growing among black folks as among white,
Kanuck, Tuckahoe, Congressman, Cuff, I give them the same, I
receive the same

And now it seems to me the beautiful uncut hair of graves.

Tenderly will I use you curling grass,
It may be you transpire from the breasts of young men,
It may be if I had known them I would have loved them,
It may be you are from old people, or from offspring taken soon
out of their mother's laps,
And here you are the mother's laps.

This grass is very dark to be from the white heads of old mothers,
Darker than the colorless beards of old men,
Dark to come from under the faint red roofs of mouths.

O I perceive after all so many uttering tongues,
And I perceive they do not come from the roofs of mouths for
nothing.

I wish I could translate the hints about the dead young men and
women,
And the hints about old men and mothers, and the offspring taken
soon out of their laps

What do you think has become of the young and old men?
And what do you think has become of the women and children?

They are alive and well somewhere,
The smallest sprout shows there is really no death,
And if ever there was it led forward life, and does not wait at the
    end to arrest it,
And ceas'd the moment life appear'd.

All goes onward and outward, nothing collapses,
And to die is different from what any one supposed, and luckier.
    [6, pp. 26-27]

In the silence my sister Sally leaned forward to say how glad she was that I decided to include that poem in the service. Keith made some closing remarks, and then it was finished. The pallbearers put the coffin in the hearse and the family walked out the door to the cars lined up behind the hearse. The cemetery was only a few blocks away, but the ride seemed to take forever. When the hearse finally stopped, the pallbearers carried the coffin to the shaded area by the gravesite.

The pallbearers and family members stood near the coffin and waited as other people joined us, forming a circle around the grave. We waited several minutes because people were still coming. I could hear the voice of the announcer coming from the football stadium one block away. It was warm and sunny; there was only a little breeze. It was a fine day for fathers and mothers to watch their sons play football. Keith thanked everyone for coming and asked us to bow our heads. After his prayer, no one moved. No one knew what to do. Finally, Jan's father walked over to shake the pallbearers' hands and to thank them. Jan and I did the same, and the crowd began to disperse. Jan invited Jason's friends to come to our house, then everyone got into their cars and drove away.

Jason's friends did come, and I was glad. They were a living connection to Jason. They had memories to share, feelings to express. They sat in the living room and Jan showed them the pictures Jason had taken during our trip to Chicago last year and the pictures he had taken at a party this past summer. They looked at the pictures. They reminisced about the party. They talked about Jason. They asked for copies of some pictures and Jan promised to send them.

As I was walking through the kitchen Sally asked what I thought when the door burst open at the funeral. I asked why she wanted to know. She had questioned several people and they all gave the same response—that it was Jason's spirit leaving. Because my parents are very religious, I expected them to believe that, but both Sally and Jan had the same reaction. This surprised me since neither of them are religious. Jan never went to Sunday School as a child or church as an adult. Religion has simply been nonexistent for her. Her attitude about immortality was that it didn't make sense to worry about it since it was impossible to prove. But when that door flew open, Jan knew that Jason had literally "blown out of there," leaving in a manner so typical of him. Before the funeral, Jan did not know how she would be able to leave the cemetery, the coffin, his body, but after this incident with the door, she knew that Jason was no longer there.

Encouraged by these comments, I explained my perception of the door as a "sign" that Jason had left the room, that he was all right. I spoke of my prayer. I had not said a word about it to anyone, but now it had to be mentioned in order to explain why I would believe that the door incident had a special significance. I also admitted that I still had doubts, that it could have been the wind. My father had been listening and he reminded me that he had walked to the mortuary with my mother, and they had talked about how beautiful the day was, how little wind. Sally agreed saying she was not aware of any wind blowing at the cemetery.

As I tried to recall what the weather was like before the funeral and at the cemetery, I realized that my father and sister were right. There had been no noticeable wind, only an occasional gentle breeze. When we stood by the grave with our heads bowed in prayer, it was so still that mosquitoes slowly drifted toward me and landed on my shirt front. Certainly there was nothing like the sequence of strong gusty winds which would have been required to move the door an inch or two, followed in a few seconds by another gust strong enough not only to blow the door open but to slam it against the outside wall.

People stayed until late in the evening. Everyone made their own supper. There was plenty of food. After the last guests left, Jan and I sat in the living room with Tess and my parents. We talked a little. Tess turned on the television and the words "Amazing Stories: The Movie" appeared on the screen. I was surprised because I had just looked at the television schedule and this movie was not listed. I explained to my parents that the movie was produced by Steven Spielberg, one of Jason's idols, that it was made up of separate stories and the first one was one of Jason's favorites. It was called "The Mission," and it was also directed by Spielberg. They had never seen the movie, so we all decided to watch it.

"The Mission" takes place on a World War II bomber. The plane becomes so badly damaged in an air battle that the belly gunner is trapped in his gun turret and the landing gear won't go down. They have enough fuel to get back to the base, but their only recourse is to "crash land" which will be dangerous for the crew and certain death for the belly gunner. The crew tries various strategies to extricate their comrade but everything fails. As they prepare to land, the belly gunner (who wants to be a cartoonist after the war) draws a realistic picture of the bomber with big cartoon-like wheels coming down in place of the damaged landing gear. As he stares intensely at his drawing, cartoon wheels appear magically on the plane which lands easily. Everyone gets out of the plane and they cut open the bubble where the belly gunner is trapped. Once out of the plane, the belly gunner continues to stare intensely at his drawing until one of the crew slaps him to bring him out of his "trance." At that moment, the cartoon wheels disappear and the plane collapses to the ground, smashing the belly gunner's turret.

My parents enjoyed "The Mission," but when it ended they said they needed to go to bed. Jan was tired so she went upstairs as well. The movie continued with a spoof of horror films which Tess insisted on watching, so I stayed up with her. I was tired, but too much had happened today for me to sleep. I poured myself a glass of wine and sat in a chair pretending to watch the movie with Tess. I was thinking about how much Jason liked "The Mission." Jason liked movies because miracles could happen. He knew it was only a fantasy, a magician's trick to distract you from the harsher world of reality, but he liked an occasional escape from reality. Illusions have their place, but at this moment I wanted a real miracle. Those are harder to come by.

Bone and Tissue Bank
Medical College of Wisconsin

September 15, 1989

Mr. & Mrs. Kent Koppelman
1017 West Avenue South
La Crosse, WI 54601

Dear Mr. & Mrs. Koppelman:

On behalf of the Medical College of Wisconsin, may I express my deepest sympathy to you and your family for the loss of your son, Jason.

I am writing to express my appreciation for the most precious gift you so generously donated from your late son.

We recovered several segments of bone and soft tissue which will be made available to surgeons, in Wisconsin, for use in transplant. The bone can be used as grafting material for patients that suffer trauma or require spinal fusions. It will also be used to replace bone affected with a tumor thereby sparing that patient an amputation. The soft tissue, which is tendon material, will be used for reconstructive purposes. In other words, the love for Jason you expressed by allowing this "Gift of Life", will improve the quality of life for a large number of people.

I know that words alone can not lessen the pain you and your family must feel, but I hope the knowledge that your gift helped so many will be a comfort to you in the future.

Sincerely,

Barry W. Duncan
Procurement Coordinator

9200 West Wisconsin Avenue • Milwaukee, Wisconsin 53226 • 414 259-3162 • 24 Hour 414 257-5405

Eye
Bank

September 20, 1989

Mr. & Mrs. Kent Koppelman & Family
1017 West Avenue South
LaCrosse, Wisconsin 54601

Dear Mr. & Mrs. Koppelman & Family:

I would like to take this time to send our deepest
condolences for the loss of your loved one. I would
sincerely like to thank you for your unselfish and
loving gesture concerning the eye donation of Jason on
September 13, 1989 at Lutheran Hospital.

I would like to inform you that the corneas were
used for transplantation. On behalf of the doctors over
the state and nation, the grateful recipients, the eye
bank and myself, thank you for helping give the Gift of
Sight to others.

If there is anything I can do or if you have any
questions, please feel free to contact me.

Sincerely,

Margaret Kelm,
Administrative Director

MK/jh

Wisconsin Eye Bank—Madison
University of Wisconsin Hospital & Clinics
600 Highland Avenue, Madison WI 53792
Telephone: (608) 263-6223

Supported in part by grants from:
Brodhead Lions Club   Mrs. Carol Pester
Consolidated Papers Foundation Inc   Tomah Lions Club
Mrs. Alma Edwards   Mr. & Mrs. William Waldon
Lions District 27–C1   Wisconsin Council of the Blind
McFarland Lioness Club   Wisconsin Lions Foundation
Madison Central Lions Club   Woodward Governor Company

Remembering with friends . . .

I tried to talk to everyone who came to our home after the funeral, but I kept returning to the living room to listen to Jason's friends. I didn't say much; I just listened. I had always tried to give Jason some privacy, particularly when he was with his friends. That is especially important for an adolescent, and it seemed a small sacrifice with a lifetime ahead of us. Now, I felt as though his friends had information that I desperately needed. They had memories with Jason that I didn't have, and I wanted those memories in exchange for a future with Jason that had been suddenly stolen from me.

What was Jason like with his friends? Was he different from the Jason I knew? To some extent, he must have been. All of us act differently with our friends than with our parents, even as adults. What was Jason like around his friends? I wanted them to tell me but I didn't know how to ask, so I just tried to stay on the periphery of the group as they sat and talked in the living room. And I tried to hear everything they said.

They talked about the trip to Washington, D.C. when they were seniors. That's where some of the friendships had begun. They talked about high school, especially "Mass Media" which was Jason's favorite class. Matt and Chuck had worked with Jason to produce a movie for their final project. It was supposed to be a spoof of "private eye" films. Matt and Jason sat in the cafeteria one day and developed an outline for the plot. Matt suggested "A Really Big Guy Named Shirley" for the title and they were off and running.

I remembered how excited Jason was because he was going to direct the film. Matt wrote the script because he could also use it for an assignment in his creative writing class. The murder occurs at the factory in the hollow tree featured in Nabisco's animated advertising, and the plot concerned corruption among the Keebler elves. Chuck was the voice of Marilyn the macho receptionist who never appears on camera, much to Chuck's relief. Matt played the cross dressing detective. Other students were recruited to play minor roles—the elves, extras and of course, "the dame." Jason appeared in the film in a small role as a victim of the homicidal elves.

They spared no expense (having little to start with) buying costumes at Goodwill and having elf hats custom made at a novelty shop. I let Jason use my office one weekend so he could film some of the scenes there. The film became an increasingly ambitious project as Jason decided to experiment with some cinematic techniques. In one scene where Matt was driving a car, Jason projected a black and white cowboy film onto a screen behind the car window to parody the obviously simulated backgrounds seen in older films.

Some ideas worked and others didn't, but Jason had a piece of good luck with the climactic scene. It was a shootout with evil elves at the "Keebler Magic Tree" with the tree bursting into flames at the end. Jason and his cast went to a park south of town to shoot the scene and found that the county was burning a brush pile, so Jason was able to have an impressive long shot of a huge smoldering pile of tree limbs. The rest of the scene was shot in a shed where Jason built a fire in an old barbecue grill and filmed the elves writhing behind the flames. That was when the "adlibbing" problem began. The "actors" kept embellishing their lines with profanity during the final shootout. When Jason shot the scene again the actors repeated the profanity.

Finally the filming was over and the editing began. This could have been difficult but luck was with Jason again. Jan had just received a new editing system for the Media Center, but she had not had time to take it out of the box yet. Jason discovered it, unpacked it and spent hours setting it up and poring over the manual. It was just what he needed to complete the film. He spent most of his Christmas vacation perching for hours on end with his nose about three inches from the video screen editing the evolving masterpiece. In reminiscing about the film, Matt recalled the "totally unfounded rumor" that Jason flunked physics that semester because of it. It was more than a rumor. I had a "discussion" with Jason about his physics grade, about going to college, about commitment. He obviously had commitments, just not the kind I wanted.

Matt remembered going with Jason one time to watch him edit. Matt had hoped to learn how to use the equipment, but it was too complicated. He was amazed at how expertly Jason mastered the video editing decks. Jason worked for three eight-hour days just to incorporate the music from "Psycho" and other movies into "his film." He had to do this during Christmas break because the movie was scheduled to be shown to the media class when school resumed. As the final touch, Jason printed movie posters on his computer ("Coming Soon! A Really Big Guy Named Shirley! See it at a classroom near you!") and Matt posted them all over the walls at school ("Read the novel from Pocket Books! Nominated for twelve Academy Awards!").

Chuck said that when they finally showed the film in media class, Jason had promoted it so successfully that the students were expecting a professional "work of art." It was not, but they still liked it, and the teacher said it was the best media project anyone had ever done for him. In the evaluation, he noted that the only reason he did not give them the highest grade in the class was due to the "excessive sophomoric language," a reference to the adlibbed profanity. Matt said the highest praise in the evaluation was for Jason's directing, especially his ability to "rise above the immature script." Matt smiled and insisted that this criticism referred to the profanity and not to the actual script (which was, of course, brilliant). Chuck said their film was shown to media classes for the next three years as an example of excellence. I thought of this conversation later when Chuck sent me a note which ended with this paragraph:

> Thinking about the fun we had making that film for media class, I can't help wondering if it is possible for me to have another friendship with someone as close as the one I had with Jason. I doubt I ever will. After all, we kind of grew up together, went to school together from fourth grade on, lived within one block of each other, and worked together at Taco John's. We didn't always appreciate each other. We had some disagreements. We drifted apart and then back together again. We shared almost everything, like we were brothers, only better—we were friends.

Another memory which generated considerable discussion among Jason's friends was the party they had the summer following their high school graduation. This was the secret party Jason had tried to conceal. It was early that summer when I began discussing plans for our annual road trip to visit family and friends and Jason surprised everyone by announcing that he wasn't going to go with us. He thought it would be better if he stayed home and kept working to earn as much money for college as he could. I was concerned that his grandparents would be upset if he didn't come, but I told him I was pleased to hear him making such a mature decision. Jason was probably thinking, "He bought it."

Jason was alone for almost two weeks. I called him once or twice, but I was sure that all was well. Jason had always proven trustworthy when he had stayed home alone before, and he was certainly not a social butterfly. He didn't even go to school dances. Like most adolescents, Jason did not share much information about his social life, but it was not terribly difficult to determine his activities because he was careless about leaving "evidence" in obvious places. I would sometimes find notes from his friends on the kitchen counter or Jan would find messages left on a pile of laundry in his room.

Jason had apparently told his friends that his parents had figured out that the party was at our house. It wasn't much of a mystery. Shortly after we returned from our trip, Jan found five polaroid photographs on the floor in Jason's room when she went to get his laundry. She showed them to me. The pictures clearly documented the festivities. One photo was of several teenagers (whom I did not recognize) lounging in our living room (which I did recognize despite the fact that the only furniture in the room was a couch and a chair draped with Jason's blue and white plaid flannel sheets). The kids in the photograph were all holding bottles containing a pink liquid, and they all looked very happy. There was also a picture of three of the same young people, holding the same bottles (the liquid at lower levels) with their arms around each other, still looking very happy. Another photo revealed two teenagers sitting on the blue-plaid covered couch in the nearly barren living room looking *extremely happy* (and somewhat surprised by the flash from the camera).

The fourth photo was of Jason wearing a red Hawaiian print bandana tied around his forehead, holding a bottle of that popular pink liquid in one hand (raised in a toast to the photographer) while he had an arm around the shoulders of an attractive girl with shoulder length dark hair. The girl looked happy, and Jason looked *ecstatic*. The fifth photo confused me at first, but then I recognized that it was the interior of our refrigerator containing an array of those ubiquitous bottles of pink liquid. As I looked more closely I could make out a label—Bartles and Jaymes. They were drinking wine coolers, and the silver container wedged onto the bottom shelf was a keg of beer!

I was stunned. Jan was outraged. We had been duped! Then we laughed. We could not believe it. It was so unlike Jason. When Jan went back to his bedroom to get his laundry, she put the photos back on the floor. Neither of us were quite sure how to handle this, but Jan argued that we should not say anything right away (like Brer Fox, she would lay low). She wanted to wait. She wanted to give Jason the opportunity to tell us about the party.

Over the next few weeks, Jan found more evidence of *The Party:* B&J caps in nooks and crannies about the house and more in the yard; cigarette butts and Tiparillo ends in the grass surrounding the patio; an empty Marlboro pack in the flower planter (. . . and Brer Fox, she *still* lay low). It was surprising to find the cigarette butts and Marlboro pack because Jason was such an adamant anti-smoker. He had been relentless in urging Jan and me to quit smoking three years earlier.

As Jason began to pack his belongings in boxes in preparation for going to college, Jan decided to provide some hints that we knew about the party. He didn't react. Since he seemed reluctant to "confess," Jan decided to help him. (Brer Fox was tired of laying low.) Not being a proponent of the subtle approach, she cornered Jason in his room and said, "Did you have a party when we were gone?"

Such a direct question evidently caught Jason off guard and he stammered for a bit and denied knowing what she was talking about. When Jan asked about the B&J caps, the Marlboro pack, the cigarette butts and the Tiparillo ends, he continued to proclaim his innocence, but finally admitted that some friends *HAD* dropped by during our absence, and they *MIGHT* have had some cigarettes and *PERHAPS* brought a few beers or wine coolers with them and he *MAY* have had one or two coolers himself. As the coup de grace Jan brought up the photographs. Jason was not surprised that she had seen them. In fact, they were still lying exactly where Jan had found them—in the middle of the floor in his room, about ten feet from where they were standing at that moment. Jason just shrugged. Obviously further denial was futile.

After a moment's pause, Jason admitted hosting a party to celebrate his birthday. He wanted to have some fun with his friends before everyone left for college. He insisted that he was very careful, that anything breakable was put away, that he moved most of the furniture into the dining room and blocked off all access to it. He covered the remaining furniture so that nothing would get spilled on it and the photographs documented this. He refused to let anyone smoke in the house which accounted for the cigarette butts in the yard. He admitted that some beer was spilled on the carpet but he had rented a Rug Doctor and cleaned it. He finished by saying that everyone had a good time and nothing was damaged. His final words on the subject were ". . . I had the best birthday ever. I've never done anything like this before. I'm glad I had the party, and I'd do it again."

Jan felt a bit overwhelmed by his aggressive defense, and reluctantly, she had to acknowledge the strength of his arguments. She agreed that he had acted responsibly in the way he handled the party, but she still didn't like the secrecy of it. She wasn't sure how to respond, and finally asked if he would at least clean up the butts and other debris in the yard. He said he would, but he never did. For a long time I continued to find a stray cigarette butt or the plastic tip from a Tiparillo or a B&J cap buried in the thatch whenever I raked the yard.

When Jason's friends talked about the party, it was clear that it was a special time for all of them. They smiled; their eyes became bright; there was even some laughter. Then they would become serious again, lost in thought. What were they thinking? Perhaps of death, or Jason, or perhaps of their own mortality. I felt sorry for them, but I also wanted them to talk more, to say more about the good times. I wanted to hear about all of the times, good or bad. I hungered for any details about what Jason had done or said or felt when I wasn't around.

I have tried to stay in touch with Jason's closest friends. They occasionally stop by when they come home. Sometimes I have encouraged them to reminisce, assuring them that they need not censor their memories. Eventually I heard about the business of making fake "IDs." For once Jason had been more careful and had not left much evidence lying around, so neither Jan nor I were aware of this particular scheme.

One of Jason's friends first began making fake driver's licenses so he and his college friends could buy beer. When he mentioned it during a phone call, Jason immediately took a strong interest in the "commercial" possibilities. Jason owed quite a bit of money to MasterCard as well as to the University of Iowa and he was in desperate need of an additional source of cash. The two of them agreed to get together over Christmas, at which time the friend gave Jason a copy of an Idaho driver's license he had made. It was not very good, but it was, as he put it, "good enough for a beer at Pizza Villa." When Jason got back to Iowa, he began to make and sell Idaho driver's licenses for $20. It was not a very profitable venture, and he still owed a large debt to MasterCard when he came home for the summer.

Jason was attracted by the easy money of the fake ID "black market," but he knew he could charge more if he could come up with a Wisconsin driver's license. Wisconsin licenses have a more complex design which makes them more difficult to duplicate. Jason borrowed a friend's Macintosh computer to recreate the Wisconsin state seal and other details, but recreating the different colors seemed impossible. While working on this problem, Jason remembered that his license was almost expired and he needed to renew it. While waiting for his photograph to be taken at the Department of Motor Vehicles, he noticed an open box of new laminates within his reach, so he grabbed a handful. The laminates had "Wisconsin" and an outline of the state printed repeatedly on them which was almost impossible to duplicate. By a sheer stroke of luck, the ability to make a perfect imitation of a Wisconsin driver's license had become a reality.

Jason purchased lumber and other materials to build a photo copy-stand in our basement. This accounted for the mess I found down there after we returned from Europe. He spent many hours at that copystand working to perfect a prototype license. He succeeded, and he had no problem finding customers. Jason began making several trips to the one hour photo shop at a shopping center. He also "lost" his license another time or two as did some of his friends, and each time the Wisconsin Department of Motor Vehicles lost more laminates. After a while, Jason began to be troubled by this illegal activity. He also knew that Jan and I would be very upset if we found out what he was doing. It was becoming a moral dilemma.

Jason talked to Matt about his growing sense of guilt. He decided to create a film about making fake driver's licenses and drinking alcohol. Matt and Jason spent several days filming with a largely improvised script. In one scene, Jason described his "recipe" for creating fake licenses while dressed as a chef. The film was intended to be humorous, but it was also a "confession." At one point Matt filmed Jason speculating on an appropriate date to show this film to his parents. He assumed it would not happen for at least three years, but a few weeks after the accident Matt gave me the raw footage. Later, Matt spent many hours editing the footage to produce something close to the final version Jason had in mind. It was a clever film, and ultimately, it made a strong statement against drinking just to get drunk.

I appreciated this "gift" from Matt, and I also appreciated the emotional price he must have paid to edit all that footage. The film illustrated Jason's sense of humor, his warm friendship with Matt, and his moral quandary about selling the fake driver's licenses. The film also demonstrated Jason's creativity. In different scenes he alluded to some of his favorite television programs such as "The Wonder Years" or "Thirtysomething." It was not a polished piece of filmmaking, but it was not intended to be. It was merely a confession and an apology. Only Jason would think of doing it as a parable presented on film.

I thanked Matt for finishing the film and told him to come back anytime. He did, a few times. We talked about films or how he was doing at college, and once Matt recalled an incident that happened after he began to date Missy. On their first date Matt told Missy that any girl he dated must meet and approve of Jason since Matt spent most of his free time with Jason. So they met, and Missy approved, and as time went on, she began to genuinely like Jason.

According to Matt, such a response was not unusual once a girl spent time with Jason. He had a gentle, easy rapport with several female friends, although he dated none of them. Matt said Jason was "too much" of a romantic, and the relationships he had with girls were more fantasy than reality, a product of his active imagination. I could believe that. I found a tape that Jason had made for someone named "Kathy." It was a selection of love songs he taped from various records. At the end of the tape was a song called "In My Dreams" and at the end of the song Jason's voice can be heard saying "Thank you, Kathy, for being in my dreams." He obviously never gave her the tape. I often play it when I'm driving alone in the car.

One afternoon while Matt was at work, Missy experienced a "crisis." She had been harassed by a stranger and she was shaken by the encounter. Since Matt could not help, Missy turned to Jason for comfort. Relying on his vast repertoire of romantic fantasies (he would probably have called them "half-vast," one of his jokes), Jason created a spur-of-the-moment "date." Even Matt described it as a date; it was probably the first one for Jason.

Since expenses had drained his meager savings early in the summer, Jason had to get some money. His standard strategy in such situations was to sell compact discs. Grabbing two discs from his ever fluctuating collection, Jason took the distraught Missy to a used record store and was paid five dollars for each. Jason once described himself as a "CD Junkie." He claimed to have purchased and resold as many as 200 discs, and Matt said it was true (but Jason and Matt both tend to exaggerate). With ten dollars, Jason took Missy to a matinee, his standard antidote for depression, despair or any other problem. "When Harry met Sally" was perfect for this purpose with its nostalgia and romance and big band melodies. Missy loved it, and by the time it was over her heart was filled with "rays of sunlight and singing birds." At least, that was how Jason saw it, but he still wasn't finished.

After the movie Jason brought Missy home where they waded through the clutter strewn around the kitchen and living room (Jan and Tess and I were still in Europe). Jason cued up a CD of big band music, they kicked off their shoes and they danced in the living room (in between glasses of wine coolers). Then Jason was seized with an inspiration. He moved the living room couch out the front door and onto the front porch. He disconnected the two enormous stereo speakers (borrowed for the summer), dragged them outside and connected their cables. After he finished, he cued up another CD, opened two more wine coolers and sat with Missy on the couch on the front porch listening to the music.

Sometime afterwards Missy told Matt how she and Jason talked of life, of distant plans, of career goals. They had looked at the pine trees, the traffic, the park across the street as their bare feet touched the cool cement of the front porch. They watched the sunset as the sky changed color and the streetlights came on. When it began to feel chilly, Jason moved the couch back inside, and Missy, with singing birds in her heart (and seven wine coolers in her blood), immediately went to sleep on the couch.

Matt would typically come over to see Jason when he got off work, usually bringing some leftover pepperoni slices if there were any. The night of the "date," Matt was surprised to find Missy asleep on the couch. Jason put his hand on Matt's shoulder and described her dreadful day and recounted his efforts to cheer her up and how important it was for Matt to be sympathetic, but when Missy woke up she felt fine. She didn't need any sympathy because Jason had already made her feel much better. When Missy told Matt what a perfectly wonderful time she had with Jason, Matt felt pangs of jealousy for the first time. All that was left to do was to take Missy home and kiss her goodnight. It was like stumbling into the happy ending of a great movie.

After taking Missy home, Matt came back to our house with mixed emotions, but then the two friends began to talk as they always did. They talked until the early morning. By the time they went to bed, Matt realized that he no longer felt jealous. By the time he was drifting off to sleep, he was thinking, "Oh well, if I have to lose my new girl friend to somebody, I guess it would be okay if that somebody was Jason . . . and we would probably still be friends."

CHAPTER 4
Searching

A man said to the universe:
"Sir, I exist!"
"However," replied the universe,
"The fact has not created in me
A sense of obligation." [8, p. 101]

Stephen Crane

My son is dead. How do I make sense of that? Where do I find meaning in the midst of such despair? I have buried a child who should have buried me. I have buried a child who should have had children. I should have had the chance to love those children, spoil them, tell them stories: stories I heard from my father; stories he heard from his mother; stories about births and burials; about loving and dying; about joy and suffering. Stories about being a family.

I was never sure where Jason's journey through life would take him, whether he would realize his dream of directing films or redirect his dream toward another goal, but one thing I knew was that he would be a good father. He had, as they say, "a way" with children. I think it was because he never lost touch with the child he once was. Children seemed to sense that in him and responded warmly to him. One of my favorite lines in the Keillor essay read at the funeral was:

"Looking at them (the stars), my son lying on my chest, I could imagine my grandchildren, and they were more real to me than Congress."

The idea of Jason's children, my grandchildren, continued to be real to me, even as his death was unreal. His death was a "fact," duly recorded in the accident report and death certificate and reported in the newspaper, but it was a fact I was not prepared to comprehend.

On Sunday, the day after the funeral, most of the relatives and friends left. "Goodbye." "Take care." "Drive safely." There was an undertone of urgency in our voices as Jan and I repeated these mundane phrases of leave-taking. There was also a certain sadness in parting, normally disguised by optimistic assumptions that we will meet again. Jason's accident had momentarily shattered those assumptions. I felt some relief at each departure because it takes energy to be with people, to be animated, to listen, to respond. It was especially difficult since I was feeling a desperate need to think about Jason, about what had happened, to form some kind of understanding. I was glad, however, that we would not be left completely alone. My parents had agreed to stay for a little while longer, and that was comforting to me.

The boxes brought back from Jason's dorm room were stacked on the back porch. Every time I walked through the porch to say goodbye to someone, I noticed Jason's red and black plaid bathrobe atop the stack of boxes near the door. It was wrapped around a pillow, and I began to picture how Jason looked in it. The image was so vivid it became painful each time I walked to the door and saw the bathrobe. Finally, after bidding some of Jason's friends goodbye, I stopped on my way back into the house and unwrapped the bathrobe from around the pillow, and at that moment I smelled something familiar. It was Jason's smell. It came from the bathrobe. I took it upstairs to the bedroom and sat on the bed. Breathing deeply, I buried my face in the bathrobe and for a moment, it was like Jason was alive, in the room with me.

I closed my eyes and lay down on the bed clutching the bathrobe to my chest, bringing it up to my face to smell it again, hugging the cloth in place of my son. Afterwards I carefully tucked the bathrobe onto a shelf of the telephone stand near my side of the bed. Just then Jan came in and asked what I was doing. I showed her the bathrobe, but I couldn't say anything. I couldn't think of anything to say. She walked around the bed and hugged me. Neither of us spoke.

I did not go to work the week after the accident. I arranged to have all my classes covered by colleagues except for one. This class would have been difficult for someone to teach with so little time to prepare. It met for two hours twice a week and I thought I could manage that. Jan had also arranged to take some time off. It was good that we did not go back to work right away. We simply did not have the mental or physical energy needed for a full day's work.

I was regularly experiencing muscle spasms which partially accounted for my sense of fatigue by the end of the day. The spasms were not painful, but while sitting or lying down, my arm or leg would suddenly twitch, or my head would jerk in response to a muscle twitching in my neck. I am not certain how often I experienced these spasms, but for a couple of weeks they occurred on a regular basis, at least a hundred times every day. I was still not sleeping well, still waking up at 5:00 every morning no matter when I went to bed. Some of my friends recommended going to a doctor to get something to help me sleep, while others offered me valium. I refused. I felt too vulnerable to be taking any kind of drugs, no matter what good purpose they might serve for the moment.

On Monday afternoon, I told my father to come with me while I ran a few errands. Once in the car, I told him I wanted to drive out to the site of the accident and asked if he wanted to come with me. He wanted to see it, too. I didn't tell him why I needed to see the road, but that was as important as my need to see the accident site itself. We drove across the bridge spanning the Mississippi River and through the small town on the other side. On the edge of the town we saw a sign pointing the way to the television station on top of the bluff.

I was prepared to encounter a steep, winding, treacherous road. I was prepared to chastise myself for not having driven on the road sooner, before Jason took the job at the television station. To be able to feel guilty about something connected to the accident seemed perversely comforting to me. Perhaps it would have been a strange sort of consolation to be able to say, "Here was something I could have done and then Jason would not have been killed." It was not to be. The road was wide, well marked, inclining gently up the bluff. The curves in the road were gradual enough to be negotiated easily except when there was ice and snow which make any road dangerous. It was easy to spot the accident site because the tall prairie grass growing in the ditch on the south side of the road was flattened out over one long stretch. I drove onto the shoulder of the road and parked the car.

It was my father who noticed the orange marks on the highway which were apparently made by the sheriff. They indicated where Jason went off the road, where the car became airborne, and where it landed in the ditch and began to tumble. There were pieces of the car and shattered glass strewn around and large gouges in the soil which the car dug out as it tumbled "head over heels." There was a large flattened area where it appeared that the car came to rest. You could see what had happened, but it still didn't explain the accident.

Jason had just gone around one sweeping curve and was approaching another slightly sharper curve. As the road started to curve again, Jason continued to drive straight ahead. He must have been distracted for a moment, or he must have been thinking of something, not paying attention. I don't know what happened, but as the road curved his right front tire drove straight onto the gravel shoulder. The tire marks suggested that he began to brake at that point, but his right rear tire was also on the gravel shoulder before he had turned the steering wheel. This is probably when the car began to skid. Jason was probably in a hurry and going a little too fast. Not much, but enough.

By the time Jason turned the steering wheel to get the car back onto the road his left front wheel was also on the gravel shoulder. It takes time to describe it, but all of this happened in a second. As he turned the steering wheel, his tires hit a paved road which joined the highway. The side of the paved road was about an inch high and his front tires slammed into it so hard that both wheel rims dug out chunks from the edge of the road. The marks were visible. The car must have become airborne, landing on the edge of the ditch and then into the ditch.

My father spotted a big gouge which would indicate that the rear end of the car must have bounced so high going into the ditch that the front bumper dug into the ground, leaving a large gouge in the soil. This was how the car began to tumble. Jason probably suffered his fatal head injuries when the car landed on its roof the first time. Jan's brothers had seen the wrecked car with its four doors still open. When the car crashed down on its top, the four car doors popped open and were jammed so tight that they could not be closed. The shallow ditch consisted of soft, loamy soil with tall prairie grass and a gentle ascent on the other side. Had the car rolled and not tumbled, or had Jason been thrown from the car right away, he might have survived, but once the car came down on the roof, he had no chance.

From what I had been told, Jason must have been thrown clear of the car during its final tumble. My father and I could not determine where he landed. After looking around, trying to understand how it happened, trying to find anything of Jason's that might have been overlooked, we returned to the car. As I started to drive toward home, my father noticed another area where the grass had been flattened several feet beyond where we thought the car had stopped. I stopped and we walked over to look at it. The grass was more flattened here than anywhere else, so we decided this must have been where the car finally stopped. I told my father not to say anything to Jan about going out to the accident site. I would tell her later, but not now.

My parents left the next morning. I was sorry to see them go, and yet I knew that if Jan and Tess and I were to reestablish some semblance of a normal family life, it must be on our own. It could not be done by or with anyone else, no matter how much we loved them or they loved us. That afternoon I told Jan about going out to the accident site. She suspected that I had gone out there. I said it seemed to help me a little to have some idea of what happened. I offered to take her if she wanted to go. She wanted to think about it. If we drove out there, she thought we should give Tess the choice to go along.

The class I had to teach began late in the afternoon. The students had been assigned material on different philosophies of education and we were supposed to discuss their implications for different teaching styles. Although it was a topic I enjoyed, the numbness I still felt made me a little nervous about being able to concentrate well enough to lead the discussion. As the students began to talk, I relaxed and gradually became more animated. I was able to enter the world of ideas and became energized by this as usual. It was a welcome relief from the numbness. It was also short lived. When I returned home I felt utterly exhausted.

This was to be the pattern for the next several days. I was able to complete various tasks in the morning and into the early part of the afternoon, but no matter how active or inactive I was, by mid-afternoon I always felt tired, incredibly tired. The evening after I taught class was no exception, I stared at the television, not really watching, and then went to bed. Clutching Jason's bathrobe, breathing deeply, grateful for the sense of smell, I fell asleep.

My parents left a check to help purchase a tombstone, so Jan and I looked at some. After a salesman explained how expensive it would be to purchase separate gravestones for each family member, we decided to get a family monument. We had to make another decision. Jan's name and mine would be carved onto the monument—in what order did we want them carved? I suggested that Jan's name should be carved next to Jason's. She had been closer to him in life, so it seemed that she should be closer to him in death as well. After choosing the color and size of the monument, we decided to have a ceramic portrait of Jason attached to it. We had seen such portraits in church burial grounds in Europe. We also wanted an epitaph on Jason's portion of the monument, a line from the Keillor essay:

". . . when you look at the stars
you don't think small . . ."

We showed the salesman a business card Jason had designed for his fantasy film company and asked if they could carve the design on the monument below the epitaph and above his name:

SURELY PICTURES
Films for Fun, Not for Profit

That was more than most people put on monuments, but Jan and I wanted it to reflect something personal about Jason, to say something about who he was and who he wanted to be. To have this was to say why we loved him.

I had not renewed my regular exercise routine since the accident. It had been a week now, and it seemed important to reestablish that, so at noon I went to the YMCA to swim some laps. There are three lanes for lap swimmers: one for leisurely swimmers; one for fast swimmers; one for those who swim at a steady pace. Although I usually swim in the latter, I thought I would start in the leisurely lane. It was a good choice. When you swim up and down the lane with no sound other than the splashing of water, there is nothing to do but think. There are no distractions. As I swam, my mind kept generating images of the accident and replaying them over and over like a silent movie. When I wasn't imagining the accident I was recalling scenes from the hospital. I could not concentrate on swimming and was unable to swim at my normal pace. The sense of moving in slow motion became even stronger. I lost track of how many laps I had completed so I didn't know when to quit. At last I simply stopped and got out of the pool. For the rest of the week this would happen every time I swam.

In the afternoon I brought the boxes from the back porch upstairs to the guest room and unpacked them. I sorted out Jason's books, putting those having to do with film and filmmaking on a shelf and setting others aside. I found my copy of *Leaves of Grass*. Jason had apparently taken it to Iowa. He had assignments written on the Table of Contents and they included the section I had selected for the funeral. It pleased me to know that he had read it. Among Jason's film books I found one which described how director Max Ophuls created a film from a short story. The book included the film script for "Letter from an Unknown Woman," and the short story on which the script was based. Because this title sounded familiar, I paged through the book and found the story. It was written by Stefan Zweig and I remembered having read it [9].

The story was about a woman who has a brief affair with a famous writer and gives birth to his child but does not tell him. Later, when the child dies unexpectedly, she writes a letter expressing her love, confessing that she was the one who sent him a rose every year on his birthday, announcing the birth and death of their child, and asking him to grieve with her for the child. The woman dies after mailing the letter and by chance it arrives on the writer's birthday. As I paged through the story I saw the part of the woman's letter which said, "My child is dead, our child." I flipped quickly past that to the end of the story and read the last paragraph. As the writer "meditates" on the letter he realizes that he did not receive a rose today on his birthday for the first time in years. "He gave a start: it seemed to him as if a door had been flung open suddenly by an invisible hand, and a cold current of air from another world flowed into his peaceful room" [9, p. 185]. Finding this line about the door was just a coincidence, I knew that, but I was still moved by it. I closed the book quietly and put it on the shelf with the books I wanted to keep.

In addition to organizing his books, I looked for any poetry Jason had written. I was happy to find enough to create a collection of writing which could be printed and shared with family and friends. It seemed like something meaningful to do. I didn't want to begin right away because it was already the middle of the afternoon and I was supposed to take Jan and Tess to the accident site as soon as Tess came home from school. They wanted to see it. I promised myself that I would work on the writing project tomorrow, but then I remembered the clutter in the basement which I had also planned to clean up tomorrow. The work in the basement wouldn't take long. I could do that right away in the morning and then start on the writing project.

While we were waiting for Tess to come home, Jan talked to me about another idea for the monument. She had a print of Van Gogh's "Starry Night" in her office, and she remembered Jason asking her the day before the accident if he could have it for his dorm room. We had bought this print when we were first married and had it in our living room for a long time. Jason said it reminded him of home. Jan's suggestion was to create a sketch based on this painting and have it carved on the side of the family monument which would otherwise have only our last name on it. The name could stay (amid the stars) with the title of Keillor's essay, "Laying on our Backs Looking up at the Stars," carved across the top [5].

I liked her idea so much I called to make an appointment with the salesman right away to discuss it with him. Jan began working on a sketch which would simplify the painting. She finished in time to take it with us when we talked to the salesman the next day. He said it could be done, but it would cost considerably more money. We had anticipated that, and we told him we wanted to have it done regardless of the cost. He promised to call us so we could look at the layouts for both sides of the monument before they carved the stone.

As soon as Tess came home from school, we drove out to the accident site. By this time I had received the accident report, so I tried to explain what had happened to Jan and Tess as best as I could. I emphasized to Tess the importance of *always* being alert when driving a car. I had often criticized Jason for not paying attention to what he was doing around the house. I always emphasized the need to be *conscious* of what's going on around you. I did not like "Walkmans" and similar paraphernalia which encourage people to "tune out" the world. The world can be a pleasant place or a dangerous place, and you've got to pay attention to it, whether to appreciate the pleasure or to avoid the danger.

When we reached the site we walked into the ditch amid the scattered debris—pieces of chrome, glass from the shattered windshield. We stared at the gouges in the earth as if waiting for them to explain what had happened. We looked for clues. We looked for anything overlooked before. We reached the wide area of crushed grass which my father and I thought was the car's final resting place, but it was not. The accident report identified it as the place where Jason's body came to rest after he was thrown eighty feet beyond the spot where the car stopped tumbling. The grass had been trampled down by the ambulance and the paramedics who had tried to save him. We stood for a while, not saying anything, then turned and walked back to the car.

We walked slowly, staying in the ditch, fighting back the tears. Suddenly Jan gasped. She bent down and stood up clutching Jason's Ray-bans against her chest. Jason loved those dark glasses. Jan was almost breathless. She said it was as if she had been told to look down at that moment, and there were the glasses staring up at her, lenses reflecting the sunlight. We looked around carefully to see if we could find anything else, but there was nothing.

It was hard to believe that my father and I had missed those glasses when we were there earlier, hard to believe they were unbroken and unmarked after the violence of the car wreck, hard to believe that they were still there a week after the accident. Jan felt certain that it was Jason telling her to look down so she would find his glasses. She was shaken by the experience, moved as much by a sense of wonder and gratitude as by the suffering that intensified even as the experience also provided some measure of relief.

LOCAL CASE NO.	**TRAFFIC ACCIDENT REPORT**	NO. VEHS	NO. KILLED	NO. INJUR	HIT-RUN	
89-001715	(POLICE USE ONLY AS REQ. BY STATUTE)	1		0	ATTEND.	UNATTEND.

DATE OF ACCIDENT	MONTH 09	DAY 13	YEAR 89	DAY OF WEEK Wednesday	TIME ☐ AM ☒ PM 2235	COUNTY Houston	☐ CITY ☒☒ TWP. LaCrescent

ROUTE SYSTEM	ROUTE NUMBER OR STREET NAME		AT ☐ INTERSECTION WITH	OR	146 ☒☒ FEET ☒☒ S	☐ MILES ☐ N ☐ E ☒☒ W OF
ON CR	Co Rd #25					

REFERENCE POINT	INT. ELEM	PUBLIC PROP DAM ☒☒ ☒	ON BRIDGE ☒ Y ☒☒ N	PHOTOS TAKEN ☒☒ Y ☐ N	ROUTE SYS. Twp Rd	ROUTE #, STREET NAME, CITY LIMITS, REF. POST, OR FEATURE T-283 Selke Road
_ _ _ • _ _ . _ _ _						

FOR DPS USE ONLY

UNIT NO. 1 - VEHICLE 1 | **UNIT NO. 2 - ☐ VEH 2 ☐ PED ☐ BIKE**

DRIVER LICENSE NUMBER - 1	STATE
K-145-4247-0259-05	WI

FIRST NAME	MIDDLE	LAST
Jason	David	Koppelman

NUMBER AND STREET (CURRENT)
1017 West Avenue S.

CITY	STATE	ZIP CODE	
La Crosse	WI	54601	608-785-0137

DATE OF BIRTH	SEX	LIC. UNDER WITHDRAWAL	WRONG D/L ADDRESS	RESTRICTIONS COMPLIED WITH	CLASS
07 / 19 / 70	M	☐ Y ☒☒ N	☐ Y ☒☒ N	☒☒ Y ☐ N ☐ NA	Reg.

FIRST NAME OWNER - 1	MIDDLE	LAST
Kent		Koppelman

NUMBER AND STREET
1617 W. Avenue S.

CITY	STATE	ZIP CODE	
La Crosse	WI	54601	608-785-0137

VEHICLE TYPE	YEAR AND VEHICLE MAKE	VEHICLE MODEL	COLOR
10	1982 Datsun	4-dr STW	Bro

LICENSE PLATE NO.	YEAR	STATE OF ISSUE	NO. OCCUP	FIRE INVOLVED	VEHICLE TOWED
EJL193	90	WI	1	☐ Y ☒☒ N	☒☒ Y ☐ N

INSURANCE CO.
Kemp Economy Ins. La Crosse, WI

(Driver/Owner/Vehicle column labels for Unit 2 are blank)

EST. DOLLAR AMOUNT COMBINED

DAMAGED UNIT NUMBER 1	HAZARDOUS MATERIAL OR WASTE ☐ Y ☒☒ N		HAZARDOUS MATERIAL OR WASTE ☐ Y ☐ N	DAMAGED UNIT NUMBER 2
EST. DOLLAR AMT OVER ☒☒ UNDER ☐ STATUTE REQ	OVER ☐ UNDER ☐ STATUTE REQ	1 REAR END 3 LEFT TURN 6 RIGHT TURN 8 HEAD ON		EST. DOLLAR AMT OVER ☐ UNDER ☐ STATUTE REQ
SLIGHT MODERATE SEVERE ☒☒ $ Total		2 OVERTAKING 4 OFF RD. LEFT 5 RIGHT ANGLE 7 OFF RD. RIGHT 9 SIDE SWIPE		SLIGHT MODERATE SEVERE $

DESCRIPTION

Veh #1 travelling eastbound on Co Rd #25, whereas the driver was travelling at a speed faster than existing road conditions would allow. This caused Veh #1 to leave the roadway on a sharp curve. Veh #1 then overturned twice causing the driver to be ejected. Driver of Veh #1 was then transported to La Crosse Lutheran Hospital where he was then pronounced dead.

OF INJURED PERSONS/WITNESSES	ADDRESS	24	25	26	27	28	29	30	TO HOSP.
Driver		1	19	M	1	3	3	K	☒☒ Y ☐ N

Remembering with family...

Going to the accident site was both painful and helpful. All three of us had walked carefully past the gouged ground, the shattered glass, the plastic pieces and matted grass, wandering among the debris of death, looking for something to make sense of it, wanting more of a legacy than a smashed car and our bruised hearts. Jan's experience was personal and spiritual and I was glad for her, but it was also an experience that could not be shared, not even in the telling of it. The only thing clear to me was that understanding how Jason died was not going to provide us with anything to relieve our suffering, to help us bear the burden of sorrow. The only thing that might do that was to remember Jason's life. When we got home we talked about that, about the qualities that made Jason special and the incidents that illuminated those qualities and shaped our perceptions of him.

For Jan, remembering Jason would always be connected to children, how he loved children and how they loved him. It was as though children recognized the child in him, grinning at them just beneath the mask of adolescence. He especially liked babies. When Jason was in middle school, he wanted to earn money by babysitting but he was concerned that people might not hire him because he was a boy. To establish his credentials, he took a "babysitting course" so people would take him seriously, and he finally got a few babysitting jobs. It was only because he needed more money than sporadic babysitting provided that he finally decided to take a newspaper route.

Jan remembered our trip to Kansas City to visit some friends. When we arrived, Jason was pleased to find a child care business going on in the home. Several children were playing in the living room when we walked in, so Jason immediately began to play with them. He was fascinated by two boys and played with them for hours. He took snapshots of all the children and asked Jan to photograph him with his two favorites. These pictures went into his photo album which already had many pictures of Jason holding babies or playing with children.

Tess said that's probably why Jason liked the Cabbage Patch dolls. When Jason was a sophomore, Jan was surprised to find that one item on his Christmas list was a Cabbage Patch doll. The request was partially a joke, but after they talked, Jan recognized that he was also somewhat serious about it. Cabbage Patch dolls had been introduced during the Christmas season two years earlier and had sold out immediately despite their price. By the next Christmas, they were not as expensive and more were available so Jan bought one for Tess, and later bought another for Tess's birthday. Jason had looked at the Cabbage Patch dolls in the store and at Tess's two dolls. Jan had bought dolls for Jason when he was little and he knew that she would have bought him such a doll if they had been available. He understood that the only reason he wasn't supposed to ask for a Cabbage Patch doll for Christmas was because of his age, and he resented that. He thought they were cute, and he wanted one.

Although initially surprised by Jason's request, Jan eventually understood it as simply another example of Jason trying to hold onto his childhood. This was an endearing quality at times, but it could also be an exasperating one. What Jan liked most about his request was that it was clearly an expression of the nurturing aspect of Jason's personality. She knew that he was a little embarrassed, but he had obviously thought about it, and this was not a flippant decision. On Christmas morning, Jason was still a little embarrassed (but also pleased) when he came down the stairs and saw, sitting amid the gifts under the Christmas tree, a red headed doll with glasses and a name tag attached to its shirt that said:

My name is Casey
. . . For Jason

One incident Tess remembered was not necessarily her favorite story, but it was Jason's. It happened the summer Jan and I went to England. We had asked Jason and Tess to go with us, but castles and cathedrals and museums did not appeal to them. Since Tess was only ten and Jason was just turning sixteen, we did not think they were old enough to stay home alone, so we made arrangements. My parents stayed with them for a few days, they spent a few days with my sister in Iowa City and then stayed with some friends who lived near Cedar Rapids. From Cedar Rapids, Jason and Tess were to fly to Boston where Craig and Sherry, our friends in New Hampshire, would pick them up and take care of them until Jan and I returned.

When Jan bought the airline tickets she told the travel agent that a ten year old and a sixteen year old would be using them. Although Jason had flown before, it would be Tess's first time on a plane. They had to fly to Minneapolis where they would change planes for the flight to Boston. The travel agent assured Jan that flight attendants would make a special effort to take care of Jason and Tess. Jan had explained it carefully to Jason—Ray and Sue would make sure they got on the right plane to Minneapolis; a flight attendant would help them find the gate they needed at the Minneapolis airport for their flight to Boston;

they would have a two hour layover in Minneapolis so they would have plenty of time to find their gate; a flight attendant would help them find Sherry who would meet them at the Boston airport.

When Jason and Tess were taken to the Cedar Rapids airport, the skies were full of dark clouds. They had no problem getting on the plane, but the plane had a problem getting off the ground. It had been raining all morning with sporadic bolts of lightning. As he sat on the plane waiting for takeoff, Jason listened to his Walkman, but periodically he would take off his earphones and ask Tess, "Haven't we left yet?" After half an hour went by he began to get nervous. He started making comments like "We're never gonna make it. We're gonna have to take a later flight from Minneapolis."

After more than an hour, the plane finally took off and Jason immediately fell asleep, still wearing his earphones. Tess remembered that she had a cold which made her ears ache when the plane came down in Minneapolis. Despite the assurances about assistance from the flight attendants, all they did was smile and say "Goodbye" when Jason and Tess left the plane. Jason decided to follow the people in front of him until he saw a monitor with information about the outgoing flights. Then he began to panic, "We've been going the wrong way!"

Jason took off running and Tess tried to keep up while shouting, "Wait for me Jason!" When he reached the people mover he stopped to catch his breath, but as soon as Tess caught up with him he grabbed her wrist and pulled her onto the people mover. He knew that the left side was supposed to be kept open for those who wanted to walk, so he walked as fast as he could, dragging Tess behind and asking people to move if they were standing in his way. When they got off the people mover Jason stopped to look for gate numbers, then he shouted, "Come on! We're almost there!"

Jason started running again, but Tess was too tired to run. Jason was moving fast and getting far away before he turned around and saw Tess walking well behind him. He ran back and grabbed Tess's backpack out of her hand and took off running again. That did the trick. Tess started crying and screaming, "Give that back!" Of course Jason had no intention of stopping so she ran after him screaming "Jason! Stop!"

When Jason reached the waiting area at their gate, he was relieved to see that the plane was still there. Then he noticed that the loading ramp was slowly swinging away from the plane. Jason spotted an airline attendant still in the gate area and shouted, "Stop! That's our plane!" Tess arrived in time to see Jason vaulting over the seats (carrying her backpack as well as his) as he ran toward the door of the loading ramp. The airline attendant picked up a phone and in a short time the loading ramp was reattached to the plane. At last, Jason and Tess were on board the flight to Boston.

Once on the plane, Jason flopped into his seat exhausted, but Tess could hear him muttering to himself. She couldn't hear what he was saying, but she was certain that she shouldn't listen. There were two nuns sitting in the seats behind Jason and Tess was hoping that they couldn't hear what he was saying either. The flight attendants acted as if nothing unusual happened, but Tess saw Jason glaring at them every time they came by. He was furious that no flight attendant had helped them as was promised. It only made matters worse when the flight attendant "helped" them at Boston. As they came into the reception area Tess saw Sherry and ran up to give her a hug and a kiss. After that Sherry came over to give Jason a hug, at which point the flight attendant demanded to see three pieces of identification before he would let Sherry take them. Finally they went to claim their baggage but there was nothing to claim; their suitcases did not arrive and would not be delivered until the next day.

After it was over, Jason seemed rather proud of himself for getting to the plane on time. He told the story to Sherry on the drive to her house and after he got there he told the story to Craig. He also told the story to Jan and me when we arrived, and Tess insisted that he was making himself more heroic each time he told it. By the time we returned to Wisconsin, the version Jason was telling his friends implied that he had practically carried Tess onto the plane! So the story became one more point of contention in the ongoing, ritualistic feud which constituted their relationship. But even Tess had to admit, it made a good story.

Tess was right in claiming this story as one of Jason's favorites. His favorite stories were almost always ones in which he had triumphed over some adversary or some dilemma, no matter how small it might be. I remembered an incident from his senior year which Tess had never heard. Jason and a friend had arranged to meet another friend who got off work at midnight. They drove to the top of a parking ramp downtown to eat snacks and to talk. They were interrupted by a police officer who demanded to know what they were doing. The officer was obviously upset, so the three young men were extremely cooperative. They answered his questions and showed him what they were eating— Oreo cookies and milk.

The officer finally asked if any of them had urinated onto the sidewalk below the parking ramp. All three vehemently denied doing this. Apparently the officer had been hit by a spray of urine while walking on the sidewalk below. By this time it was obvious that the officer was not going to catch the person who had done it. He demanded to see their identification. Since Jason and one of his friends were only seventeen, the officer issued citations to both of them for violating the city's curfew ordinance for children under eighteen.

Jason was quite upset that the officer had taken out his anger on two innocent people. In Jason's view, all three of them were "good kids" who didn't smoke or drink or take drugs, and yet by being in the wrong place at the wrong time, two of them were going to be punished. Jason and his friend planned to go to court and argue their case before the judge. They decided not to tell anyone about the citations. To keep their parents from knowing, they intercepted the official letters notifying the parents of this incident.

When it was time for their day in court, Jason and his friend dressed up in slacks, sport coat and tie. When their case came before the judge, they were nervous but maintained a semblance of calm as they explained what had occurred. After they had finished, the judge commended the young men on their appearance and on the maturity they demonstrated in presenting their arguments. Although they had technically violated curfew, he decided to waive the fine because no apparent malice was intended.

Jason was elated over the successful outcome. When he came home he immediately described the entire incident to me. He had fought the foe on the field of battle and emerged victorious. He had triumphed over injustice! He and his friend had argued on the merits of their merits. They were not criminals and they had behaved properly; they had been socializing not vandalizing; they had done no harm nor had they intended any. They had persuaded the judge by these arguments and he had ruled in their favor. They had relied on our system of justice, and the system worked. It was satisfying moment for Jason, and I couldn't fault him for feeling jubilant. A just resolution of any problem in such an uncertain world is reason enough to rejoice.

For several days after this conversation I thought about incidents I remembered from Jason's life and the "Jason stories" others had told me. Such stories recalled small events, insignificant stuff, not the stuff of great literature but certainly the stuff of human life. When families share such stories, they demonstrate their intimacy with the person in the story while reinforcing their intimacy with each other. These stories may make us laugh or smile or cry, but they all say the same thing—here was a life. In this way, stories become a celebration unmatched by any fourth of July spectacle. We must remember such stories. We should tell them more often than we do. Each story is sacred testimony to the life of a human being, to all humanity. We have lost much of our sense of what is sacred in the modern world. We need to search for it if we are to have any chance of discovering it again.

CHAPTER 5
Doing

And then—the watcher at his pulse took fright.
No one believed. They listened at his heart.
Little-less-nothing!—and that ended it.
No more to build on there. And they, since they
Were not the one dead, turned to their affairs. [10, p. 171]

Robert Frost
"Out, Out . . ." [10]

"There was nothing I could do." Sometimes the pronoun changed to we or he or she, but this refrain of helplessness haunted me. I had to believe there was something I could do. Even though Jason was dead, there had to be something I could do for him, the way I had always tried to do things for him when he was alive. I didn't know what I should do yet, but I would do it as soon as I knew what it was. Jan and I decided to contribute the money we would have spent on Jason's college expenses to his scholarship fund. We met with a woman from the foundation receiving contributions to tell her how much money we could contribute each year and to ask about the amount required before the fund could actually award scholarships.

The woman explained that all contributions in Jason's name were presently being added to an existing scholarship fund. Although the foundation would keep a record of the contributions for Jason's fund in a separate account, the interest from these contributions would be added to the interest generated by the existing fund and added to the scholarships awarded in the spring. Jan described our plan to donate Jason's college money to the fund in order to create an independent fund. We wanted to award scholarships in Jason's memory to students who planned to major in film or broadcast journalism in college. We understood that it would take several years before we would have accumulated enough money for the account to function as an independent fund issuing scholarships.

Although Jan and I were committed to this long term goal, I needed to do something more immediate. I thought I could complete the task of compiling Jason's writing in a few days so I was anxious to begin. When I got up on Thursday morning, one week after the accident, my plan was to clean up the mess in the basement and then start working on the writing project. I went downstairs to the kitchen and started the coffee maker. I assumed that the basement task would take about twenty or thirty minutes. When I was finished I would have a cup of coffee and begin to read and organize Jason's writing.

When I got down to the basement, I looked around to see what had to be done. It wasn't too bad. Jason had left some tools out; he had littered the floor with some newspapers and cardboard. He must have been sawing some lumber since there was sawdust and several pieces of wood on the floor. It was so typical of Jason. He would always get involved in a project and then just walk away when he was done, leaving the mess for someone else. "Someone else" was usually Mom or Dad. Looking around, I began to recollect all the times I had nagged him about "another mess" I had cleaned up for him. A thought began to rise up slowly, imperceptibly, until it struck with the force of an ocean wave—I would never have to clean up after him again. This was the last time I would have to do it.

Tears welled up in my eyes and my body started to sag as if a sack of cement had just been thrown onto my shoulders. I knew that I could not stay in the basement. The accident had erased Jason from my life, leaving only traces of him. This was one of those traces and I could not remove it, not yet. I stood there for some time just staring, imagining Jason covering the floor with the paper and cardboard, imagining him sawing the wood. I went upstairs to the kitchen. The coffee was done. I poured myself a cup and went into the living room to sit down on the couch.

I was still sitting when Jan came downstairs. She knew of my plans for today so she was surprised to see me there. She asked me why I wasn't in the basement, but I could not find the words to describe what I was feeling. She sat next to me and hugged me, and I wept as I tried to explain. In the end I said I would probably be able to clean up the basement after I finished the writing project, because I would have created something in memory of Jason. Jan told me not to worry about the basement, and we sat for a little while, helplessly holding each other.

Later that morning I looked through all of Jason's papers. Most of them were homework assignments. Among the math lessons and history essays from high school, I also found three poems Jason had written for English class—a love poem, a humorous poem, and a poem about buying popcorn at the movies. Among his college papers I found more poetry. These poems had been written for himself and not necessarily for a class. In them, he expressed feelings of isolation and loneliness and occasionally nostalgia. I was familiar with most of these poems because Jason had previously shown them to me. He was quite proud of them, and so was I. It was both joyful and painful to read them again. They whispered promises of what was to come, of the sensitive, loving, caring young man taking shape in the mind of that big boy's body, a body so casually battered and a mind so quickly crushed in that roadside ditch, retracting the promise of the man by taking the life from the boy.

In addition to the poetry, I found a short story and the papers he wrote for his college literature classes. I particularly liked the paper on the epic poem *Beowulf* [11]. He described how Beowulf gave credit to fate for his victories, but that the poet gave Beowulf credit for being bold and daring. Jason wrote that Beowulf had gained much because he was willing to risk much, and that those who don't risk have no chance to be rewarded by fate. These comments reflected a new direction in Jason's thinking.

When he was in high school, Jason openly talked about his belief in "fate." This had not surprised me. As a high school English teacher, I found this to be common among adolescents. To believe in fate is to eliminate having to take responsibility for one's choices. It promotes the idea that it doesn't make any difference what you choose to do because fate will determine the outcome. Jason and I had discussed "fate" on several occasions. I argued that people do have some control of their lives, that a person can shape his or her life and give it meaning and that the main factor determining the outcome was not "fate" but the resources and opportunities available to the person.

The paper on *Beowulf* suggested that Jason was beginning to see risk-taking as an important factor for success; that fate or luck did not solely determine the outcome. Now he was dead, and his own death was largely due to bad luck, which some might call "fate." Whatever it was that distracted him occurred where the highway curved so if you drove onto the gravel shoulder it would be more difficult to get the car back onto the highway. The paved road which happened to join the highway at that point probably caused the car to become airborne which increased the likelihood of the car going into the ditch. Jason went into the ditch (not too steep, but steep enough) at a speed (not too fast, but fast enough) sufficient to cause the car to tumble end over end rather than roll from side to side. Once the car began to tumble, there was little chance that he would survive.

All of these factors combined to cause Jason's death. Change any one of them and there might have been no accident or Jason might have walked away from the crash or at least survived with injuries. Others have done so. As Marilyn had said, "If everyone died whenever they did something stupid, there'd be no one left alive on the planet." Jason was one of the unlucky ones. He did not survive his mistake, but his accident was not fate. It was simply another reminder of how fragile life is. If there was a lesson to be learned, it was how important it is to be conscious of the dangers around us, how vigilant we must be to protect our lives and those we love. And lurking behind this lesson is the thought that we might still be hurt or killed no matter how vigilant we are. The truth of such a lesson is not a pleasant one to contemplate, but we must remember another truth, that the odds go up significantly if one is careless.

As I continued to search through Jason's papers, I found the journal he had kept during his trip to England with the high school marching band. He had written something every day for the ten days he was there. The band trip ended in London, but Jason went on to Bonn to join other students from his German class for a three week stay with families of those students who had come to Wisconsin the previous summer. Jason did not like his German experience. He wrote almost no journal entries while there, and the few that he wrote were quite negative.

I didn't want to use any lengthy writing. I decided to use excerpts from Jason's journal, almost all of his poetry, and the short essay he wrote for his college entrance exam. The essay was humorous, providing some balance for his poetry which tended to be serious and often sad. I organized the writing in a sequence which revealed a variety of moods. I used part of a "Last Will and Testament" he had written in his journal to conclude the writing. Jason apparently had thought about his own death as he took his first transatlantic flight. The conclusion of his will said:

Thank You, All. It was an interesting life.
Goodbye, Farewell, Amen

A long time ago, in a galaxy far, far away . . .
. . . there was Jason

Tess had written a poem for Jason two days after the accident and had shown it to me. It was a good poem. More importantly, it said something about Jason and his dying that spoke for all of us in the family. I wanted to use her poem at the end. The poem spoke of love and it said goodbye. It seemed an appropriate way to conclude the collection.

My growing pride in Jason's writing resulted in the development of a more ambitious plan for this project. Initially I had only intended to duplicate a few pages for friends and relatives, but now I wanted to create a booklet using a good quality of paper, large sheets folded in the middle and stapled with a cover of thicker stock. Jan liked the idea. She proposed a design for the cover and suggested using Jason's high school graduation picture on the first page.

Since I had finished with organizing and editing Jason's writing, I printed the pages and gave them to Jan. Some people at her college found out about this "project" and offered to donate the paper and allowed Jan to use their equipment to duplicate copies. Jan ordered copies of Jason's graduation picture for a total of fifty booklets. Jan and I developed a list of family and friends (including some of Jason's former teachers) who might appreciate the booklet.

While I was going through Jason's writing, Jan had been going through boxes filled with his clothing and personal items. She tried to decide what to keep and what to give away. This was not easy. Jan packed some of Jason's things in boxes, but she wanted certain items, objects of some significance to Jason, left in the "guest room." When Jason went to Iowa City, Tess moved up to his bedroom because it was larger than hers. Her old room became the guest room, and Jason was our most frequent "guest." It was his room when he came home for Christmas and during the summer. I think he would have preferred to stay in his old room, just for the space if not the sentiment, but he accepted the logic of Tess taking his room since he was now a more temporary resident.

I had worried about Jason's reaction to losing "his room." Even though he seemed to accept it, I was not certain how he really felt. As an adolescent, Jason had been guarded about his emotions. He had been shy as a child, and he continued to be shy. His public persona was quiet, impassive; he seldom made eye contact or had much to say. With his family or his friends he could be playful and exuberant, but he became more reserved once he entered high school. I knew this was not unusual for a "teenager," but it made communication much more difficult.

Jan and I had been worried about Jason's self-confidence because of his less than successful first year at college, and now being back home attending a small college. We insisted that he move into the dorm, only a few blocks from our house, rather than live at home. Jason agreed to this, but we were afraid he might secretly feel rejected and resentful. When he moved into the dorm in August, Jason was glad that his roommate seemed quiet, even a little shy. There were many freshmen in the dorm but they respected Jason because he had already completed a year of college. He seemed comfortable in his dorm, enthusiastic about his classes, and excited about his job at the television station. Jan and I felt an enormous sense of relief. Everything seemed to be working out. Now all that remained were a few of his things in "his room."

Jan arranged Jason's mementoes around the room—his high school diploma and graduation tassel, a replica of an Oscar statue, an old radio microphone, some stuffed animals, his Indiana Jones hat, a few movie posters. On the window seat sat Casey, Jason's Cabbage Patch doll. Jan had selected Casey because his hair color was similar to Jason's and so were his glasses. When Casey's glasses were broken, we teased Jason that this was proof of his "parentage" because Jason was always breaking his glasses. My contribution to Jason's room was to sort and shelve his books and videotapes. It seemed important to have a part of our house belong to Jason, to connect him to us. I often come to this room to write, surrounded by his things, feeling the emptiness of his absence.

Organizing Jason's writing had been a satisfying task, but it was finished and I wanted to do something else. Jan had made a suggestion earlier about writing to some of Jason's heroes, like film director George Lucas. He was one of a small number of people in the film industry with whom Jason felt "connected." My interest in her suggestion may have been influenced by the Zweig story in Jason's book. Like the woman in that story, I wanted to tell them about Jason's death as if I were introducing my son to people he admired. I also wanted to thank them for the positive role they played in his life.

I did not feel that writing to strangers was inappropriate. What was the worst that could happen to them? If they were sympathetic enough to feel a sense of loss and to mourn for Jason, it would only be a temporary feeling. It would not be a burden they would bear forever. Our civilization might be more civil if we paid attention to the lives that are lost, the dreams that die with them. We don't ask "for whom the bells toll;" we don't even hear the bell.

Jan had mentioned one or two names when she first suggested writing letters, but when I said I wanted to do it, we began to think of all the people whom Jason admired. We compiled a list of seven people who were probably most important to Jason, including writers, directors, film reviewers and one composer who had written scores for many of Jason's favorite films. Although I wanted to write the letters, I also thought it was a little crazy. These people were celebrities who must receive thousands of letters from adoring fans, but I also remembered Marilyn advising me to do crazy things if it would help. I thought this would help me, as long as I took my sense of satisfaction from the letter writing itself, and not from any expectations about receiving responses.

I thought carefully about what I wanted to say in the letters. It seemed most important to explain why each person was important to Jason and to thank each one for enriching his life. I would explain that I was writing the letters to help me cope with his death, and I would assure them that they should feel no obligation to respond. I decided to mention Jason's scholarship fund in case any of them felt they wanted to do something, but I would emphasize that this letter was not a fundraising scheme. That would trivialize my purpose and demean Jason's memory. I would assure the recipients of these letters that I had no expectations for them. My main purpose was to share a sense of who Jason was, what his life had been like and what it might have been, and the part they had played in all of this.

I wrote the first letter to George Lucas. I included an essay Jason had written for his high school English class about seeing "Star Wars" for the first time. I wanted Lucas to "hear" Jason's words and understand how much his film had affected this young boy. My favorite part of the essay was the description of the beginning of the movie when the words *"A long time ago in a galaxy far, far away"* came on the screen:

> That phrase in the quiet was chilling. It faded as quickly as it came on. I relaxed for one split second. The next moment I jumped. STAR WARS was plastered all over the screen, accompanied by the loudest explosion of music I had ever heard. The logo drifted back

only to be replaced by a scrolling introduction. For my younger mind and eyes, it went too fast for me to read, so my dad read it to me. There must have been many other kids in the theater, because during that introduction much murmuring was going on from other fathers reading it to other kids.

I remembered reading the words to him, but I did not remember hearing other parents also reading to their children. It was a wonderful image. I hoped Lucas would like it.

George Lucas was not only the first recipient, he was the first to respond. In a letter from his secretary, written less than a week after my letter had been mailed, he expressed his sympathy and also sent a "Star Wars" poster. He had signed the poster and above his signature he had written "May the force be with you." The letter explained that such posters had brought as much as $1000 or more in fundraising auctions, and I was to consider this his contribution to the scholarship fund.

Jan and I were certain that we would receive no responses from such busy people. When we saw the envelope with the "Lucasfilm" return address, we were surprised. We knew Jason would have loved the poster, but we also felt we should honor the instructions to sell it and use the money for the scholarship fund. Although the letter proposed an auction, Jan suggested a raffle with tickets selling for $1 each. I liked the idea because it gave everyone a chance to win the poster rather than making it available only to those who could afford to spend $1000. Jan said if Jason were alive he would have been ecstatic about an opportunity to get a signed "Star Wars" poster and would probably have spent several weeks worth of his allowance for tickets. To have a memento for ourselves, Jan took photographs of the full poster and close ups of Lucas's signature. She planned to enlarge the best ones and frame them with the letter. She wanted to hang it in the guest room with the rest of Jason's mementoes.

The letter to Garrison Keillor was the most difficult one to write. Because of Jason's enthusiasm for Keillor's *We Are Still Married*, I read the book before I wrote to him [5]. I enjoyed the book, but it included two essays concerning the unrealistic expectations fans can have for celebrities. Although both essays were humorous, they forced me to reconsider this letter I wanted to write. I finally wrote because I believed I was sincere about having no expectations for a response. I wanted to emphasize this point to Keillor, so I wrote about Jason and about how much he liked Keillor's work before I wrote about the accident. And then I wrote the following paragraph:

> I confess to seeking help in dealing with his death. I don't know what else to do. I have also read *We Are Still Married* now, and I found some comfort in it. I read things that I know Jason must have liked in such pieces as "Who Do You Think You Are?" [12]. and "The Old Shower Stall" and "Lonely Boy." I also read parts that make it difficult to write to you. "Meeting Famous People" and "My Life in Prison" demonstrate the craziness that fame can bring and the unrealistic expectations that people can have about celebrities. I don't want to cause anyone any pain. There is enough to go around.

I went on to say that Keillor should feel no obligation to respond to this letter. He had given Jason joy, and that was primarily why I had written to him, to express my gratitude for that. Although Jason's death was the catalyst for the letter, I was not attempting to avoid grief by pushing it onto someone else. That would have been a futile goal. Sharing grief with another may appear to reduce one's sense of grief, but it is only an illusion of relief. For that reason, it helps, but only a little, and only temporarily.

As Jan and I struggled with our grief, many people tried to be helpful. We returned to work when we felt ready to resume that part of our lives, but we weren't prepared for some of the "help" that was offered. We expected to encounter people wanting to express their sympathy, and we appreciated this, but some wanted to go beyond expressing a few kind words. They would tell us about a relative who had lost a child or some other story of loss, of pain, of suffering. They meant to be consoling, but it did not help us to know that others suffered. We were suffering, and it was all we could do to deal with that.

Such conversations could have helped Jan or me at some point, perhaps in a month or a year from now, but not now. Our wounds were still raw, still throbbing. If being at work was to help the healing process, then we needed to be able to focus on the tasks to be done. It did not help to force us to focus on our loss; if someone wanted to express sympathy, a brief comment or a simple hug would have been enough.

There was a support group in our community for parents who had lost a child, but neither Jan nor I wanted to attend. I could appreciate why it might help some people to talk about their child who died and express their sense of loss, but Jan and I talked about Jason with each other and with family or friends. It was helpful for us to talk about Jason with people who knew him. We didn't want to talk to people who primarily knew and cared about us and our pain; we wanted to talk with people who knew and cared about Jason.

Jason's friends said they felt the same need to talk about him with people who knew him, but they were all at different colleges where no one knew Jason. When they tried to explain who Jason was and what he meant to them, people would merely listen politely. That didn't help, so they stopped trying. Jan and I felt sorry for them. To struggle with grief in such isolation was obviously not easy. We knew how important it was that we could talk with each other and with Tess. We told Jason's friends to visit us and talk with us, to consider it an open invitation. We assured them that it would help us as much as we hoped it would help them.

After I had finished writing the letters to Jason's "heroes," I began to write about Jason and the events which had occurred since his death, not for anyone else, just for myself. Jan also wrote a little, and we both began by writing about the same thing—the night we went to the hospital. Writing was an attempt to organize our pain, perhaps to have some control over it. For the first few days the pain had been almost overwhelming, and I felt as though I was treading water in a storm tossed sea. The pain eventually diminished, but it would return sporadically with an almost overpowering intensity. It would strike without warning, an invisible predator.

When I began to write, it seemed to make my suffering tangible, to give it form and shape. I began to think of my pain as a monster. If I could make this monster visible, I might be able to capture it in a web of words. Although the monster would be as terrible as ever, capturing it might allow me to choose the times when I was willing to do battle with it. After I had written several dozen pages, I would occasionally go back and reread what I had written, often revising certain parts as though I had found a weak place in the web in need of repair. Once mended, I could walk away from it. Writing became my attempt to manage the pain, because there was no way to be rid of it.

October 5, 1989

BATESVILLE CASKET COMPANY INC.
BATESVILLE INDIANA 47006
812-934-7500

Mr. Kent Koppelman
1017 West Avenue, South
La Crosse, WI 54601

Dear Mr. Koppelman:

Please accept our most sincere sympathy on your recent loss.

In memory of your loved one, we have arranged for a tree to be planted in a National Forest to serve as a Living Memorial. This is accomplished in cooperation with the Forest Service, United States Department of Agriculture, as part of a major endeavor to reforest the United States. This thoughtful request was made on your behalf by Sletten, Mc Kee, Hanson Funeral Home.

Although we cannot determine the exact location of the tree, you can be assured it will be planted where the need is greatest, its species and location carefully selected by the Forest Service. We know you share with us the hope that this tree will grow in full measure to bring beauty to the landscape and pleasure to all who pass its way.

Again, we extend our sympathy and feel certain you will find peace and comfort in the knowledge that every detail of the service was properly handled. The enclosed certificate acknowledges the fulfillment of the Living Memorial.

Sincerely,

Robert H. Irwin

Robert H. Irwin, President
BATESVILLE CASKET COMPANY, INC.

Remembering to heal . . .

Organizing Jason's writing had given me a sense of satisfaction, but a sense of frustration as well. He had not written much. That's not surprising. How many of us feel a need to write our stories? How many of us think that such stories might have some value? Even if people recognize the value such writing would have for loved ones after their death, how many of us think we might die tomorrow or next week or next month? Without some sense of urgency, most people are not likely to make a special effort to commit thoughts or feelings to paper, or write narratives to describe some memorable incident from their everyday lives. Jason was simply being like most people.

Since Jason had not written much, I wanted to make up for that by requesting stories from others. I thought about my grandmother who was a wonderful storyteller. She often reminisced about her life as a young girl on a farm in the midwest. Her stories told of love and marriage, of births and deaths. Some were comic, others tragic. My cousin and I tried secretly to tape her once, but the tape recorder malfunctioned. She died before we could try again. I remembered her stories, but they were better the way she told them. They were her stories, and no one could tell them as well.

I asked Tess if she could remember any stories about Jason other than the airport story. Could she remember something he had done or something that had happened to him? At first she could think of nothing, and I realized that Jason had seldom shared much information with her. She finally remembered something. It happened the summer when she was six years old. She was in her lime green swimming suit "with turtles on the front" and she was running through the sprinkler. She wanted to make a "slip-n-slide" with plastic garbage bags but she needed Jason's help to do it. Jason had biked over to the Amoco station on the corner to buy some candy and had not returned. She went over to get him.

As Tess walked up to the front of the station she saw some boys pushing Jason and calling him names and kicking his bike. Jason just stood there. Tess remembered getting angry at the boys and marching up to them yelling—"Stop picking on my brother!" She pushed one of the boys who was kicking Jason's bike but he only shouted—"Get lost!" Not knowing what else to do, she screamed something at him and ran home.

Jason didn't come home right away, but when he did Tess saw that he was crying. He was walking fast as he headed toward the house, so she called out—"Who were those boys, Jason?" Jason wouldn't answer so she ran after him and even followed him into the house repeating her question until he reached the door to his room at the top of the stairs. He slammed the door in her face and through the door she heard him growl, "Leave me alone."

Her story made me wonder why one of the adults at the gas station didn't intervene and tell the boys to go home. The man who took over the gas station since then would have done so, and so would the people he hires. They are good people. They sent flowers to the funeral. Such simple things we could do for others, especially children, but we don't take the time. This would often upset Jason. I remembered an incident that occurred the summer after Jason finished seventh grade. A younger boy who had taunted Jason during the school year continued to harass him that summer. Jason was in the front yard when the boy rode by on his bicycle. He shouted some insult at Jason and then headed for the baseball field across the street.

Jason went into the house to phone his friend Joe. He had had enough of this name calling and he wanted to do something a little intimidating to make the boy stop. When Joe came over, the two of them rode their bicycles across the street to look for the boy among the handful of spectators in the bleachers watching the baseball game. The boy saw them coming. He jumped on his bicycle and rode away with Jason and Joe in hot pursuit.

The boy rode to a house nearby where he found about ten of his friends. All of them had their bicycles. The boy rode toward them shouting furiously to get their attention. When Jason and Joe saw the other boys they turned around and tried to get away, but they were not fast enough. The pursuers became pursued. The pursued decided to split up. At the next intersection, Jason and Joe went in different directions and the majority of the pursuers followed Jason who was riding hard for home. As he was rounding a corner, the rear wheel of his bicycle skidded on some gravel. Jason and the bicycle crashed to the street.

Before Jason could do anything, the boys were on top of him, kicking and punching. They would not let him up. At first Jason was scared, but he saw a man across the street unloading groceries from a pickup truck and he assumed that the man would help him. When the man finally looked over at the fight to see what was going on, he shouted encouragement to the boys beating up on Jason. After some time had passed and it became obvious that the boys were not going to stop until someone made them, the man came over and chased the boys away.

Later that day when Jason told me what had happened, he admitted that he had given the boys good reason to chase him. Although he had not intended any real harm, he did not blame them for what they did. He had probably been hurt more by falling off the bicycle than from their kicks and punches, but his face flushed an angry red and his eyes filled with tears of rage when he described the man's behavior. Jason kept repeating, "But he's an adult!"

If the man had simply ignored the fight, Jason might have forgiven him, but to encourage it! Jason could not understand that, and he could not accept it. He was outraged, and I said he had a right to feel that way. He had a right to expect rational, mature behavior from an adult. I can imagine some people smiling at the naivete in such a statement. I plead guilty to idealism. I could not live in a society that did not at least attempt to promote idealistic expectations for human behavior. Despite this experience and others, Jason always expected adults to "do the right thing." He continued to be surprised and disappointed whenever they did not.

During a visit to our friends Ray and Sue, we reminisced about the days when we first met back in Nebraska. Sue recalled an afternoon when she took care of Jason so Jan and I could go to a movie. After Jason had been playing for a while, he took out his box of crayons and spread them out on the carpet next to his coloring book. He had only been coloring for a few minutes when Sue noticed what he was doing and asked him to take his coloring book and crayons to the kitchen table. Jason looked up at her and said, "Why?" The bold way he asked the question surprised her, but Sue explained that he might accidentally color the carpet and then she would have to clean it, so it was safer to color on the table. Apparently that sounded reasonable, so Jason promptly picked up his crayons and coloring book and moved to the table. Sue laughed as she ended the story saying that she would always remember the nonchalant way this three year old questioned an "authority figure."

Sue's story reminded Ray of how often Jason could talk and act in very adult ways even as a small child. I asked him to write down some of these stories and send them to me. A short time after our visit I received a packet of stories from Ray. This is my favorite:

It was summer. Sue and I were expecting a visit from Jan and Kent and Jason. They were supposed to arrive on Saturday around noon. On that Saturday morning I was struggling out of sleep while Sue was saying urgently, "Ray, someone's at the door.

Someone's coming in." We never locked our doors when we were home. According to the alarm clock it was only eleven so I didn't think Jan and Kent would be here yet, but from the living room of our small apartment, Jason's clear, happy voice called out, "We're here!"

"We'll be right there," Sue called out, but then she realized that Jason might come into the bedroom and both of us were naked. Sue tried to disappear into the mattress, pulling the covers over her, but I leaped up, grabbed a pair of running shorts and had one leg in them when Jason opened the door and walked in. He stood there looking a little confused until I said, "Jason, please wait for us in the living room." After he left I finished getting dressed and went into the living room. Jan apologized for Jason coming into the apartment without knocking. She said that they were early because Kent had some books to trade at a used book store and she and Jason did not want to go with him. Jason was so happy to see us that I didn't want to spoil it for him so I decided to say nothing about his coming into the bedroom without knocking.

After Kent came, he and I sat at a card table drinking cokes and talking. Jason was used to our conversations. He would listen for a while, not interrupting, and when he had heard enough he would wander away to find something else with which to entertain himself. The card table was exactly the right height for Jason to place his elbow on it and prop up his chin; he listened in a very adult pose and with an interested expression on his face.

At a pause in the conversation, Jason asked if he could ask me a question. I said he could. "Why do you and Sue sleep naked?" My first thought was that parents should choose the time and method of telling their children about sex. I looked at Kent, but he just sat there with a smile on his face. I considered telling Jason a little white lie but decided against it. Jason took everything adults said seriously, remembered it, and judged how much to trust them by the honesty of their statements.

"Well, Jason, when a man and a woman love each other, they like to sleep naked together." Jason asked why. "Because they can cuddle and hold each other, and it just makes them feel very good and very loving toward each other." I looked at Kent, concerned that I might be infringing on a parent's prerogative, and was pleased at his unobtrusive nod of approval.

Just as I was congratulating myself on having found an answer which avoided specifics but still told the truth, Jason said, "But when you come to our house, you don't sleep naked." This was true. When we visited Jan and Kent, Sue and I would sleep in the living room on their couch which folded out into a bed. I said, "Sue and I don't sleep naked when we know that other people are around and might see us."

This gave me an opportunity to talk about the need to knock on doors before entering a room, especially a bedroom. "Remember Jason, you were early so we weren't expecting you yet, and you came in *without knocking*." I made sure to stress the last two words. In a very adult fashion Jason said, "Well, we're friends, aren't we?" This was so endearing that I just laughed and said, "Yes, we certainly are, and I hope we always stay that way."

*   *   *

Sometimes what you remember about someone is not a conventional story based on a single incident, but an ongoing situation with some thread that winds its way throughout the various encounters, connecting a variety of scenes, moments, events. This began to emerge in Jan's stories. The link for many of her memories was money, a fairly common "thread," I suspect. I asked her to write down the experiences, trying to connect all of the parts into one continuous narrative. She did, and she presented it to me on my birthday. This is her "gift":

Jason was a financial wizard; he a had a highly developed skill for making money disappear. Although he was excellent in math, he was never able to fathom the intricacies of a checking account and he never saved a dime by his own volition.

When Jason was about eight he got a job delivering papers. My part of "his" job was to help him pay the bill once he collected from his customers. Most people paid regularly, but there were always a few problem customers. Because of this, Jason didn't like to collect, and I had to hound him to do it. In addition, he didn't keep good records and spent the money he collected as fast (sometimes faster) than it came in. I had to put my foot down.

I told Jason that if he was going to keep the paper route, he would have to turn over any money he collected to me and I would pay his bill, save some, and give him some to spend. This was fine with him as long as he had enough money for Hot Wheels cars, Star Wars action figures and trips to McDonald's. He usually did, and I also saved over $100 for him in one year (which he later spent on a stereo).

After we moved to Wisconsin, Jason eventually got another paper route. Although he hated getting up in the morning to deliver the papers, he enjoyed having the money to spend on whatever he pleased. I thought he was probably mature enough by now to collect and pay his bill. Big mistake! He rarely had enough money when it was time to pay the paper. He couldn't understand it. How could he make all those deliveries, and collect all that money, and end up short by $50 or $60 dollars or more? He wanted to quit the paper route because he thought he was losing money on it!

I explained that he was buying newspapers from the publisher and selling them to his customers. Although he paid the newspaper $60, he collected over $100 from his customers, making a net profit of $40. Jason conceded that on paper the explanation made sense, but he still insisted that he was barely collecting enough money to pay his bill, leaving only a few dollars for him to spend. In fact, the real problem was that Jason was spending the money he collected (as soon as he collected it) on a variety of things, and that was why he never had enough money to pay his bill.

Jason's fiscal confusion continued. When he was almost fourteen, I decided that a checking account might help him understand his finances better. I went with him to open an account. He made his deposit and ordered his checks. I showed him how to record deposits and checks and how to balance the checkbook against the bank statement. This worked for a few months, but then Jason started procrastinating about writing down his checks and he would forget to make his deposits on time. After he received his fifth overdrawn notice in as many months (with a $10 penalty for each), I decided that this was not a good idea and we closed the account.

Jason's career as a newspaper carrier ended his junior year in high school when he got a "real job" at Taco John's. He gladly gave his paper route to his sister, who also proved to be incompetent at handling money. I began to wonder if this was some kind of genetic disorder! Anyway, Jason asked me to put him on a budget. He thought that since he would be getting an actual paycheck at predictable intervals, he ought to be able to control his spending and even save some money. He knew he needed to save a considerable amount because he was planning on taking several trips, including a summer trip to England with the Marching Band and from there he would go on to Germany with his German class. I told him I would pay all of the basic expenses, but it was his responsibility to save for his spending money.

Jason's plan was to turn his paychecks over to me. I would put a certain amount in his savings account and give the rest to him for his spending money. The system worked beautifully (even though he always complained that he never had enough money). He saved the money for his trips and even had enough to buy a ten-speed Schwinn bicycle. He was amazed at how thrifty he had become! Of course, when he went to Europe he spent every dime he took with him, and then some.

Before he went to Europe I gave Jason a credit card to use in case of an emergency. I opened the MasterCard account in my name, listing Jason as the co-holder. I made sure Jason understood that it was to be used ONLY in an emergency, and that he would pay for any purchases he made with it. I knew I was in trouble when I received a credit card call from O'Hare airport in Chicago only hours after bidding him farewell. While waiting for his next flight, Jason had decided to experiment with the card "to see if it worked." I was sure I had created a monster—a seventeen year old kid running around Europe with a credit card in my name! After I hung up, I consoled myself with the thought that there was a credit limit on his card of $1000. It did not turn out to be as bad as I feared, but Jason discovered the cash advance system which accounted for most of the $200 bill that came after he returned from Europe.

During Jason's senior year he decided to open a checking account again. After all, next year he would be going away to college and he would have to manage his own finances. I reminded him that people can be sent to *JAIL* for writing bad checks, and Jason assured me that he would be careful. Once again everything was fine at first, and then about once a month there would be a thin envelope from the bank addressed to Jason. I tried to make him understand how much money the overdraw charges were costing him (a $10 service fee for each check). I recommended that he close the account, but he decided to keep it, and his management seemed to improve.

When he went away to college, he opened another checking account in Iowa City which included a TYME card. More overdraw notices. I had given him the MasterCard, reminding him that it was to be used for emergencies **ONLY**! At first there were no problems, but before long bills arrived with charges from Musicland and other businesses that do not deal in the stuff of emergencies (by my definition).

In our many discussions about managing his finances, Jason would readily admit that he was, as he put it, "an idiot about money." I agreed with him. He told me several times that he was going to have to make it big in the world so that he could afford to support his spending habits. In the meantime, the bills kept coming. I finally got so frustrated I began to send the MasterCard bills directly to Jason with instructions to pay them **NOW**! By this time he had been hired to work at a movie theater and could afford to support his spending habits.

When Jason came home from college in May, I confiscated the credit card, but before we left for Europe I gave it back to him with strict instructions. I talked about maturity and responsibility. I suggested that he close his checking account and hide the MasterCard. He told me he'd think about it and again admitted to being "an idiot about money." I was encouraged by the fact that he was aware of his problem, but he needed to find a way to manage it.

After returning from Europe, I went to the credit union to make a deposit and the manager greeted me and asked about the trip. During our conversation she discreetly mentioned that she had called Jason about the MasterCard account (she knew we were gone and noted that there had been several transactions, but no payments). After she called him, Jason came right in and turned the MasterCard over to her and told her to "lock it up." He also admitted to her that he was "an idiot about money".

When I went home, I asked Jason about this incident. He said he hadn't been able to make many payments over the summer and he decided that it would be best if he didn't even have the card around to tempt him. He also told me that he had closed his checking account and was operating on a cash-in-hand basis. I congratulated him. We're making progress, I thought. He not only acknowledged the problem, he had taken some steps to correct it. I was proud of him.

*   *   *

Jason and Matt had been friends since sixth grade. Jason not only liked Matt, he envied him in a way. Once on a bus going to school a bully taunted Matt and finally said, "How would you like it if I smashed my fist into your face?" Matt pretended to think about it for a few seconds and replied, "No, I don't think I would like that at all." The bully laughed and left Matt alone. Jason would have given anything to have been able to remain cool like that, but he never could. In such situations he would be so overwhelmed by his feelings (fear, rage, frustration . . .) that he would be unable to think of anything to say, certainly nothing clever or amusing.

Jason liked Matt's sense of humor and they both loved movies. Their friendship deepened as the years went on and they spent hours together watching films at the theater or at home on the VCR. They became very analytical about what worked and what didn't work in a film. They would discuss the appropriate use of music, the quality of the special effects, the interesting camera angles. It was no surprise to anyone that both of them planned to major in film when they went to college, but instead of enrolling at Iowa, Matt opted for Montana State. They called each other and got together often during vacations, and especially throughout that last summer.

I wanted Matt to write for me, to share his sense of Jason with me, especially since Matt writes a story better than he tells one. In person Matt can be quiet, almost bashful. If he tells a story it is a straight narrative with few embellishments, but when he writes he seems to feel more comfortable expressing himself, to give his sense of humor free rein, to reveal his emotions. He sent me several wonderful stories, and he concluded with this one:

The weekend after Jason's parents came back from Europe and ten days before the accident, Jason and I took a road trip to Iowa. The plan consisted of visiting three friends who went to different Iowa colleges before I had to leave for Montana to resume my own academic career. It was a good weekend. We picked up Chuck at the college in Waverly and drove on to Des Moines where we partied at a frat house with Steve. The last leg of the journey included returning Chuck to Waverly and visiting Missy at her college in Decorah.

Luther College in Decorah is situated between the bluffs of the Mississippi River Valley and the Iowa cornfields. Jason and I came tooling down the highway into Decorah and promptly got lost in this twelve street town. I experienced a "whopper fit," but no Burger King was to be found. We ate at a McDonald's which had a sign saying "Velkommen!" and pictures of Viking boats on the walls. Jason noted that Leif Erickson had apparently discovered Decorah first and then discovered North America as an afterthought.

Jason and I finally found Luther College and then we hunted all over campus for Missy's dorm. When we finally found it we were told that Missy and her roommates were at a Freshman orientation dinner, so we left a message on her door and went for a walk. We didn't walk far; I was too insecure to go exploring after being lost for an hour in a town you could throw a rock over. We walked about twenty paces to a stone picnic table where I dramatically spread out on top of it to look up at the trees and the sky. Jason sat down on the bench and tilted his head back to look as well.

"I see piles of white cotton balls and white cotton candy blowing in the sky!" I gasped. For Jason, my sprawling on picnic table tops and acting stupidly awe-struck was commonplace. Awe-struck stupidity was my specialty.

"No you can't!" Jason countered, mimicking the coldly rational people of the world, "The trees are in the way!"

"Oh really? What do I see then?"

"Mobs of green people with green hair waving green banners and standing on a great blue carpet."

"I suppose they all have dark brown poles coming from their heads that one by one come together and form a barky trunk-like thing."

"You lost the spirit of the image there toward the end."

"Well hell, you're the poetic one."

"No I'm not, I hate all poetry . . . "

Since Jason had been writing a lot of poetry, this surprised me. I turned my head to look at him, my cheek resting on the table top.

". . . except for mine!" He finished triumphantly.

"Up yours."

"And yours."

I got off the picnic table and we walked back to Missy's room, all the while telling each other who, where, how, and what power tools we should try to have sex with. I figured this was the height of male bonding.

We met Missy and drove around Decorah with her, learning the names of all the places we had seen earlier. We rented a motel room and unloaded our stuff, then went back downtown and parked the car. As we slowly walked around, Missy and I held hands and Jason walked ahead and behind us, orbiting us as we strolled. He jumped around and climbed on things like we were sheep and he was a Border Collie. I couldn't shake this image as I thought about what Jason was thinking:

"Whatzit like to have a girlfriend Matt? Whatzit like? Huh? Huh? Whatzit like? (Pant Pant Woof!)

"Not baa-aad Jason, not baa-aad."

By the time we returned to the motel room we were all tired. Jason fell asleep on the recliner chair and Missy and I were soon asleep as well. The sound that woke me up the next morning was a loud static noise, like the winds of the Sahara whistling through a bamboo shoot combined with the congestive breathing of Darth Vader. This was Jason snoring. Sometime during the night Jason had slipped out of the recliner and was lying on the floor with a blanket wrapped around him.

"Let's wake him up," Missy said smiling. She flopped over the side of the bed so that her face hovered over Jason's, her mouth inches away from his snoring lips.

"What are you . . . " I whispered and strained to see what she was doing. She leaned forward and licked Jason's cheek. She continued to moisten his strawberry-blondish cheek fuzz, stopping once to ask me if I'd like to join her.

"Well, uh, no thanks." I said, but it set me thinking.

I would have liked to lick his face. I had licked many-a-face in my day, but they all belonged to girls. I tried to picture myself next to Missy licking Jason's fuzzy chin, nothing sexual about it, just licking his cheek with the same kind of affection that an older brother gives with a noogy-rap, a snake bite, or a wedgy. Of course, by the time I had expended this much thought on the subject, Jason was coming out of dreamland. He let out a startled snort upon awakening and finding this magnified face giggling and licking his cheeks.

We spent the morning together, ate lunch, and then it was time to leave. When we got to Missy's dorm, Jason stayed in the car so I could be alone with Missy to say goodbye. I'm not very good at that. I always feel like I'm saying the wrong things. I did promise to write and I gave Missy a hug, reminding her that we had promised ourselves not to be mushy and maudlin with public displays of affection.

When I returned to the car, Jason had a distant smile on his face, like he had a plan. Missy was standing on the curb, brushing her long black hair from her shoulder, waving goodbye. Jason looked at me slyly and began to hum a melody. We slowly pulled away from the curb and Jason increased the volume of his humming. Suddenly I recognized the song as the theme from the movie "Terms of Endearment."

A goofy inspiration overcame me as he sang the melody. In the spirit of the moment and completely forgetting my promise to Missy, I unbuckled my seat belt, spun around and climbed up on my seat. Missy was still watching the car as I pulled my upper torso through the sunroof, standing on the seat with my knees against the head rest. The car was accelerating as I shouted "Goodbye Melissa! Goodbye! Ciao!" I could see Missy putting a hand over her mouth and I knew she was giggling. I brought my fingers to my lips and blew her the biggest kiss of my life as Jason continued to sing the familiar theme music. Missy snatched at the air and pretended to catch the kiss.

"So long! Farewell! Auf Veederzayne!" I shouted like a fool as I waved my arms. Missy turned away and walked back to the dorm. I guessed that she was pretty embarrassed, but she later told me that she was actually a little misty-eyed. She was away from her family for the first time, and with Jason and me leaving and all that. I squirmed back into my seat and refastened my seat belt. Jason looked at me sheepishly, still quietly singing the theme. I could hear the swelling of the orchestra and violins off in the distance. He had me in that spell for a few moments more.

Jason D. Koppelman had smelly feet. He weighed about 240 pounds. He wasn't a poet (yet), he was a dabbler. He dabbled in poetry, in filmmaking, in writing, in life. He was just beginning to carve his name in the bleachers, but he could infect you with his passion. I still feel confused and angry. I still want to kick something. It's as if the world of fantasy and movies and literature—the world Jason and I embraced as a better reality—opened up and sucked one of us away. He should be sitting next to me in his car, in a movie theater. Where is he now? On the other side. The other side of the screen. I feel like I am standing in the smoke of a rocket that was just launched, and there is nothing to fill the blasted hole in the ground.

CHAPTER 6
Healing

Pain has an element of blank;
It cannot recollect
When it began, or if there were
A day when it was not.

It has no future but itself
Its infinite realms contain
Its past, enlightened to perceive
New periods of pain. [13, p. 89]

Emily Dickinson
Selected Poems and Letters

I tried hard to accept Jason's death, but I was not prepared for the difficulty of doing so. It was like clambering up a steep earthen slope whose topsoil kept crumbling beneath my feet. I would make a little progress, but then I would become distracted and slide back into fantasies of a future which included Jason. At such times I would make myself remember the scenes from the hospital or the funeral as though bending down to grasp at crumbling clods of reality to slow or stop my downward slide. That would work for a while, and I would seem to make progress up the slope, but I could only contemplate a reality without Jason for a short time and then I had to let go of it. The stench of dirt and death would fill my nostrils and I would have to stand upright and smell a purer air, free from mortal dust, sliding back down into denial.

Doing things for Jason and for myself helped a little, getting back to work helped a little, but I still struggled with the feeling of being underwater, still experienced sporadic muscle spasms, still awakened at around 5:00 every morning, still felt exhausted by the middle of the day. On the Wednesday morning of my first week back at work, two weeks from the date of the accident, I woke up and did not have to look at the alarm clock to know what time it was. I felt desperate. As I lay there, thinking, the words that had come to me on the morning of the funeral returned, "Ask, and it shall be given you; seek, and ye shall find; knock, and it shall be opened unto you." For the second time since the accident I decided to pray.

I began by apologizing for praying only when I needed help. My excuse was simply my pain. I whispered the words in the darkness of the bedroom. I spoke of my need to grieve for Jason, but confessed my weariness from the burdensome weight I felt every hour of the day. The mental alarm clock rousing me from sleep at 5:00 every morning also took away some of my strength and energy. My prayer was a plea for help, not only for me, but for my family. Jan and Tess needed me, but I was not able to do much for them because I was so physically exhausted when I came home from work. I begged for help, for something, anything to allow me to cope with my son's death, to grieve and yet to sleep. I needed to feel sorrow but I did not need to be oppressed by it. I asked for some measure of peace to relieve the constant aching in my heart.

Afterwards, I rolled over and tried to rest for a while before getting up, a routine response ever since I had begun to awaken regularly at this hour. I would usually lie in bed for twenty or twenty-five minutes or sometimes longer, still unable to sleep, and then I would get up.

I walked downstairs in our house and when I reached the bottom I heard noises. I walked past the living room and into the kitchen where I found two young men wearing vests and cowboy hats and nothing else. They were jumping in and out of a metal washtub half full of water. I tried to think of a reason for them being there, and I had a vague recollection of hiring them to entertain the children at Tess's birthday party. This was strange because Jan and I were not in the habit of hiring entertainers for our children's birthday parties, and certainly not this sort of "entertainment." I walked back to the stairs intending to shout up to Jan to ask what she knew about the two naked men in our kitchen.

As I passed by the living room again it had dramatically changed. Instead of the familiar dark terracotta colors of the carpet, curtains and wallpaper, I saw a room brilliantly lit by sunshine streaming through an open window with white lace curtains puffing out in a gentle breeze. Near the window was a brown wooden upright piano (possibly an organ) with another instrument (perhaps a guitar) lying on top of it. I did not pay close attention because I heard voices and immediately recognized them, especially one of them. I turned to look in the direction of the voices and I saw Jason! He was standing with his back toward me as he talked to his friends Matt and Chuck. They were discussing some scheme which involved hiring a Christian rock group and renting an abandoned church in town for a concert. Jason and his friends often concocted entrepreneurial schemes. Because this mundane conversation was so typical of them, I was convinced that Jason's accident and death had merely been a dreadful nightmare and now it was over. I felt a powerful surge of emotion and energy racing through my body.

As the three friends talked, I entered the living room, keeping my distance from them, but coming around Jason's side so I could see his face. He was wearing a bright blue hat with a round flat brim, a flat crown, and ball fringe hanging down from the edge of the brim. I was reminded of the hats worn by rancheros in the old Zorro television series. It seemed odd for Jason to be wearing such a hat and I wondered if perhaps the accident did happen and he was wearing the hat to cover the scars from the accident. As if in response to my thought he took the hat off and flung it like a frisbee. I could see his auburn hair and his full oval face, a little thinner, but not much. He looked so handsome! The other two boys ceased to exist for me as I focussed my attention on Jason. I looked at him with an intensity impossible to describe. It was as though my vision surrounded him, caressed him, pulled him toward me.

In the midst of this euphoria, an unwelcome idea rose to the surface. I didn't "hear" it; the only voices I heard were those of the boys. It was simply a thought intruding upon my joy saying, "No Kent, this is a dream." And I knew it was true. There was too much strangeness for this scene to be real. As I reluctantly accepted the thought, I also decided to make the most of my dream while it lasted. I rushed up to Jason with my arms open anxious to hug him and tell him I loved him.

I suspected that my attempt to hug Jason was the reason I awoke since this had happened to me before in dreams. I promised myself that I would not make this mistake again. If I ever had another dream with Jason in it, I would be content to look at him, to enjoy the illusion of being with him again. I would not demand more than that.

Jan was awake so I told her about the dream. When I described the ending I began to weep, and Jan put her arms around me and held me for a while. Despite the tears, I retained a sense of the euphoria I had felt in the dream. I had seen Jason, and he looked just like he did when he was alive. I could not hope for more than that. I was grateful for the dream, grateful to have had the illusion of seeing him. When someone you love has a terminal illness, you have a chance to make amends, to say you love them, to hug them, to say goodbye. When you are confronted with a death that is unexpected, grieving becomes a process of saying goodbye to someone who isn't there to hear you. It is a more complicated process; I am not sure how it ends.

I had another busy day ahead. I went downstairs to make some coffee and to work on grading papers. I worked steadily through the morning and did not seem to feel as tired as I usually did. Before long I realized that I did not have the feeling of being weighed down which had made me so weary. I swam laps at noon and came home for lunch. I still did not feel tired so I continued working through the afternoon. I taught class late that afternoon and came home for supper without the sense of exhaustion I normally felt by this time of day. After supper I worked at the computer for two more hours. I could not account for this sudden burst of energy. Weeks later I asked my doctor about this. He said the symptoms of fatigue which I described were commonly associated with depression. Research was still less than adequate for a thorough understanding of brain functioning, but he said it was theoretically possible for a dream to stimulate a chemical reaction in the brain which could temporarily relieve someone of some symptoms of depression. He compared it to the effect of getting a surge of adrenalin.

From that day on, I continued to cope with Jason's death, with the intense pain that could suddenly strike. The deep sense of sadness persisted and there were moments of anger, but I no longer felt as if I were constantly carrying a heavy burden or that I was walking underwater. This was what had been draining my energy. I was still tired by the end of the day, but I did not experience that physical exhaustion which had previously left me with only enough energy to stare absent mindedly at the television until I went to bed. I would still awaken occasionally before the alarm clock went off, but there was no pattern now. The effect of the dream was not to resolve my grief, but it gave me a chance to function adequately. Although my prayer had been answered, my rational mind wanted to claim coincidence. What mattered most at the moment was the enormous sense of relief I felt to be free of symptoms which had preyed upon me for the past two weeks.

For many years I have worked with educators to explore the value of human diversity and to recognize how diversity can benefit society. I had made commitments months ago to present a keynote address and to conduct workshops during October and November. I decided not to cancel anything. I wasn't sure if I could be effective, but I was certain that it would only add to the damage done by this senseless tragedy if I did not continue to work on these issues. I hoped that the workshops might even be good for me. I have enjoyed teaching for almost twenty years and I have always enjoyed working with teachers. When the time came to participate in these events, the response of the teachers gave me a welcome sense of usefulness which I needed to offset the sporadic feelings of helplessness and sometimes rage.

Rage was an unusual feeling for me. I had read about people experiencing anger in response to a death—anger at the person for dying or at themselves or someone else—so at first I was prepared for such feelings, but they didn't come. Anger has never been a frequent emotion for me, and certainly not rage, but eventually I did feel an emotion which I could not immediately identify. In the past, if I was angry I might get loud, perhaps even pound on a table and typically the anger would dissipate. Now it was different. More and more I seemed to be irritable. At first I thought this irritability was due to my increasingly busy schedule or my difficulty with sleeping, but that wasn't a satisfactory explanation. I was getting upset over trifles. When my students skipped class and did not inform me, I would feel a tightening in my throat. My son was dead but I was here. I had a better excuse than any of them for not wanting to be there, but I had come! Where were they?

This was part of it, and I don't know whether to call it anger or rage, but it was real. It was undeniably rage I felt when I read newspaper articles about rapists or child molesters, or even when I observed young men shoving each other or bullying someone. Jason would never have raped anyone, nor intentionally hurt anyone, so why were they alive while he was dead? I had no satisfactory response and there certainly wasn't anyone I could ask, so I kept that rage hidden. I especially tried to conceal it from my students and colleagues.

The lack of answers meant I had no release for the feelings of rage. The strength of these feelings began to diminish only when I forced myself to recognize the futility of my questions. My son was dead because his car went onto the shoulder of a highway at a particular place which caused it to go into a ditch and tumble in a particular way which made his death inevitable. Such things happened. It had happened to my son. That was all there was to say.

It was slightly after 6:00 on a Monday evening near the end of October when Jan received an unexpected phone call. Jan had never liked answering the phone, and now, haunted by the memory of the phone call on the night of the accident, she was even less inclined to answer it. Since I was on campus teaching a class, Tess answered and then called Jan to the phone saying, "It's some guy for you." The caller asked a few questions to make sure he had the right number and the right family, and then he said, "This is Garrison Keillor calling from

New York." We had mailed his letter just two weeks ago. Jan was stunned and afterwards could not remember many details of the conversation. She remembered Keillor saying he had a son who was also named Jason, and she remembered his suggestion that he could come to La Crosse and give a benefit performance for Jason's scholarship fund. He also said he would be sending a letter to us. When Jan hung up the phone, she noticed that they had talked for twenty minutes.

On Friday of that week, we received his letter which began:

> Dear Kent and Jan,
> It's awkward to address strangers by their first names but grief makes relatives of us all and I do join you in your grief for your boy. I have a son named Jason, who is twenty, and it is not so hard to imagine the cold empty feeling and the tears and the terrible guilt I'd go through.

He enclosed two *New Yorker* articles where he wrote about his son and enclosed a donation for the scholarship fund. In his letter he requested a picture of our son, so we sent him a copy of the booklet with Jason's picture on the first page. Jan and I were touched by Keillor's kindness and generosity. His phone call and his genuine concern provided a momentary diversion from our relentless struggle with grief. I do not do it justice to say it was merely a diversion; it was a moment of healing. It provided a rare and welcome sense of relief.

Jan suggested that we tell no one about Keillor's offer to do a benefit performance for the scholarship fund. If something happened to prevent him from coming, some people (especially the press) might perceive his generous offer as insensitive. Whether Keillor performed or not, he had done more for us already than we had any right to expect. We decided to tell people that Keillor had called us in response to the letter that I had written, but we gave few details.

Time passed. The accident and the death of my son seemed to fade from the memory of my colleagues and students. That was logical, but for Jan and me, this event and its aftermath were still vivid and our emotional wounds had not yet healed. People stopped suggesting that we come over or go out with them, and that was all right because if we needed to talk we knew there were people we could ask—people who cared, people who would listen.

One day I had an opportunity to talk to a colleague who had also lost his son two years earlier. He had called shortly after the accident to express his sorrow and to suggest that we ought to get together sometime to talk. On this particular day, I felt like talking, about his son, about my son, about grieving. I told him about the dream with Jason. He said he had also had a similar dream, but not until six months after his son's death. I could not imagine how he could have kept working for six months without experiencing the relief that my dream had provided. He had talked with other men who had lost their children and they had all had similar dreams.

His comment made me wonder how often we encounter others (acquaintances, strangers, or friends) without realizing what they have suffered, are suffering. This reminded me of a quotation attributed to Socrates—*If all our misfortunes were laid in one common heap from which everyone would be required to take an equal portion, most people would be content to take their own and depart.*

Although our friends and colleagues returned to "business as usual," most also maintained a certain level of sensitivity to the grief that Jan and I still felt. On occasion, someone would try to decide what was "good for us" without letting us decide for ourselves, and that usually created a problem. Most of these incidents were minor. The worst one involved a woman who asked Jan to bake a birthday cake for a troubled young man. She knew Jan always made special birthday cakes for our children, so she thought Jan would enjoy creating a uniquely decorated cake to make this birthday special for the young man. For Jan, this request triggered memories of all the elaborately decorated birthday cakes she had made for Jason, and with that memory came the realization that she would never again make a cake for him. Although it hurt her to refuse, it was more painful to think about doing it. Jan was in tears as she hung up the phone.

I was so upset I called the woman immediately. I was calm as I talked. Although it was two months since the accident had happened, for Jan and me it still felt as if it happened yesterday, and that was why her request was both inappropriate and insensitive. The woman assumed that baking the cake might make Jan feel better. I reminded her that Jan and I had always been willing to help others, but we were the ones in need of help right now. (I heard the echo of Marilyn's voice in my words.) We were not able to do more than we were already doing. It only added to Jan's distress to refuse to help someone. The woman apologized, and I was glad that I had called her, but the damage had been done.

Friends had advised us to get away from home over the holidays. Prior to Jason's accident, Jan and I had planned to visit my parents at Thanksgiving, and we decided to make the trip. It was both painful and helpful. On the long drive to Nebraska I kept thinking of Jason, of how he would have insisted on driving so I wouldn't get so tired, of how much he enjoyed driving, of the accident. I felt better after we arrived. I have always enjoyed being with my parents, being in the home I knew as a child. Nostalgia was part of it, but it also had to do with returning to the slower pace and the sense of security and comfort which comes from living in a quiet village.

Our two families used the Thanksgiving visit to exchange Christmas gifts. I gave my parents a VCR and a copy of the videotape Jan and Jason had made for Jason's high school graduation. The videotape consisted of still photos beginning with Jason's baby pictures and ending with his high school graduation picture. Jason had selected the music to accompany the photos. As Jan connected the VCR to the television set, I thought of Jason. While we were gone last summer our VCR wasn't working right so Jason disassembled it. According to his friends, he had parts of it strewn all over the dining room table. He had not been able to fix it, but he said he had learned more about how a VCR worked. He even managed to use most of the parts when he reassembled it. I knew Jason would have insisted on connecting the VCR for his grandparents, and after he had finished he would have patiently explained how to use it.

Such thoughts came constantly, making my sense of Jason's absence the most memorable part of this Thanksgiving. There was warmth and affection, good food and laughter and love, but in the midst of it all something was missing, a grey lining in our silver cloud. Everyone felt it. I could only acknowledge it silently and go on. We talked about Jason, of course. We talked about the good memories and how much we missed him, but I could not overcome the strange feeling I associated with Jason's absence. It was like a black hole, a force without substance, threatening to draw me into its darkness and its silence. It connected to my pain and pulled me toward it. To succumb was dangerous because there would be little hope of escape. Resistance meant to talk of Jason and affirm the value of his life, brief as it was, to speak of a past that included Jason and a future that would not. I had to accept both realities. It was something all of us needed to do.

We drove back to Wisconsin on Saturday, and at noon on Sunday some of Jason's friends came over. They had come home for Thanksgiving and were on their way back to college. They had been to the cemetery and had seen Jason's monument. After they left, Jan and I drove to the cemetery. Among the plain stone markers of varying sizes and shapes, the elaborate carving on our monument was eye catching. The side with the picture based on "Starry Night" had been skillfully carved to emulate Van Gogh's stars and moon glowing above the pine tree which leaped like a dark flame up to the sky. We were pleased. Jason would have liked it.

Walking around to the other side, I stared at the epitaph for Jason and at his name and dates carved in stone. I had been avoiding the cemetery because the grave had seemed barren without some kind of marker, some acknowledgment of who was buried there. Seeing the monument with Jason's name and picture on it was a tangible testament to the finality of his death. He was gone. There were no loopholes. The dates said it all: Born July 19,1970—Died September 13, 1989. I had to walk away as tears streamed down my face.

I had tried to do things Jason might have appreciated. I had tried to do things to cope with his death. All of it helped and nothing helped because what I wanted was for Jason to be alive again. Would that feeling ever go away? Standing by his grave, reading the words on the monument, I began to consider the possibility that the pain might be permanent. My only consolation was the thought that the pain was a measure of my love. If I felt little or no pain only two months after Jason's death, what would that say about my love for him? What would it say about me as a father, as a human being?

After Thanksgiving we received a call from Garrison Keillor's manager, Jennifer Howe. She called on Monday evening so I was in class again, but Jan talked with her. Keillor had shown her the booklet of Jason's writing, and she had been moved by it, especially by some of the poetry. Although she was certain she had never met Jason, she said his face seemed familiar to her.

Jennifer and Garrison had come up with possible dates for the benefit. Jan had checked on available dates for the auditorium in the Fine Arts Center at her college. The most suitable date was Sunday, March 25, 1993. It is difficult to describe how Jan and I felt after receiving Keillor's compassionate and generous offer, and impossible to express our gratitude adequately. I suspect he would describe his actions as an ordinary human response to a family's sorrow, but there is no question in my mind that he is an extraordinary human being.

Now that the date was determined, it seemed appropriate to share this special news. We called our parents first, then we told others. In addition to raising money for the scholarship fund, I also hoped the benefit would be a healing experience for the family. When I talked to my mother, she confessed that she still had not been able to read any of Jason's writing in the booklet. Although she had always been calm and supportive, Jason's death obviously hurt her more than she could say. I hoped that the Keillor benefit would help her, and all of us, in healing the wounds created by Jason's death. Such healing would represent a contribution far outweighing whatever amount of money would be raised. It might provide some measure of mercy to a family benumbed by death.

Garrison Keillor   Jason Koppelman

'Lake Wobegon' comes to La Crosse

The friendly folk we've come to know and love in mythical Lake Wobegon are coming to La Crosse to help ease the pain of grieving parents.

Garrison Keillor, creator of the radio show "A Prairie Home Companion," is bringing Lake Wobegon to the Viterbo College Fine Arts Center on Sunday, March 25.

The benefit is for a scholarship fund set up by Kent and Janet Koppelman in honor of their son, Jason, who died in a car accident last September.

Keillor comes in answer to a letter sent by the Koppelmans in which they told Keillor he was one of Jason's heroes. The letter so touched Keillor that he called the Koppelmans and suggested doing the benefit. Tentative concert time is 3 p.m.

Tickets range from $15 to $25 and are first being offered to the faculty, administration and students of Viterbo College and the University of Wisconsin-La Crosse since Jason's parents work at those two schools. If tickets remain, they will be made available to the public on March 19.

Thomas Reinert, director of the Fine Arts Center, says that with the donation of performance and facilities fees, it is possible the benefit would raise more than $15,000. The money will be put in a fund for Central High School students planning to major in film or broadcast journalism.

Along with the Keillor benefit, the Koppelmans also will be raffling off a "Star Wars" poster signed by George Lucas. The Koppelmans say they would like to hold the raffle at Central High School, Jason's alma mater.

■ Jason's parents remember him and share his poetry / A-6.

Reprinted with permission from *La Crosse Tribune,*
January 30, 1990, La Crosse, Wisconsin.

Remembering to love . . .

For Jason, Jan and me, the family monument linked our names in death and noted the place where our bodies would lie next to each other in time to come, but I wanted to sustain a link with Jason now. I wanted to keep my love for him alive while I was alive. To do that, it would be necessary for me to be the caretaker of his stories, not only the ones I knew but the ones others told me. I have said that my grandmother was a good storyteller. The reason she was good had to do with love. Her stories were portraits of people she cared about. Even when the people were described in death or amid some sorrow, their image would be framed with love. Listening to her tell her stories was like listening to love songs.

Love songs. I have often listened to Jason's tape of love songs as I drive around town. The girl for whom he made them never got to hear them. Perhaps she would have been embarrassed by the gift. Love is embarrassing. It makes us do foolish things. Although I knew the tape was not made for me, I still think of it as a gift from Jason.

Most of these songs reflect some aspect of Jason's personality. One boy sings about being too shy to tell a girl he loves her; another singer promises to care for his love and protect her forever; another dreams of their love lasting into the future for as far as he can see. All of the songs are dreams of love, and Jason loved to dream. Some of the songs on this tape seem almost meant for me, especially the song where the singer mourns for a lost love, a love he thought would be there "forever." He took his loved one for granted and now that she's gone, he is desperately unhappy having to live without her [14].

I know the singer is referring to a woman he has loved and lost, but his despair seems overstated in reference to a romantic relationship. People fall in and out of love; people marry and divorce and fall in love (forever) with someone else; widows and widowers find another to love (and so they should). The words don't seem realistic until I relate them to my feelings for Jason, and then they are painfully accurate. Why don't we have more songs about loving a child, loving a friend, loving a parent or grandparent. Why this obsession with one kind of love as if it's the only one that matters? When I began to write my "Jason stories," I did not want to idealize or romanticize him. I wanted to portray him as I saw him, but of course, I saw him in the light of love. The stories that follow are my love songs, love songs for my son.

*   *   *

Jason was only eight years old when he got his first job—delivering newspapers. He was under the minimum age, but the newspaper representative said Jason could have the route if Jan or I would agree to be responsible for making sure the bills were paid on time. Jason begged us to say yes. Jan worried that he was too young to do it alone, and that worried me too because if he couldn't do it I would probably have to help him. I was teaching two classes as a graduate assistant at Iowa State in addition to taking classes to complete my doctorate. I was busy enough and did not want to be given any more tasks (or any more stress).

During the week the route would not be a problem because it was small and the paper was an evening edition. Jason could deliver them after school in less than twenty-five minutes. There was no Sunday paper, but on Saturday mornings about 200 *Shopper's Guides* had to be delivered to everyone living in our section of the university's married student housing development. Jan agreed to take responsibility for the bookkeeping and Jason asked a friend to help deliver the Saturday papers for a share of the profits. With these arrangements made, Jan called the newspaper office and told them "we" would take the route. This was a prophetic comment, because it certainly did turn out to be "our" paper route.

When the first small bundle of newspapers came on a Monday afternoon, Jason was excited. He brought the bundle into our apartment, cut the plastic strips, stuffed the papers into the bag provided by the newspaper and went off happily to deliver them. He had no problems during the first week, but when several large bundles of *Shopper's Guides* arrived that first Saturday morning, it became obvious that we had all miscalculated. Although Jason and his friend each had a wagon which they loaded with papers, it took several trips and over three hours to deliver them. Jason's friend decided this was too much work. He took his share of the profits for that day and quit, leaving Jason to find someone else for next week. Someone else was Dad.

At first I protested, but I relented in the hope that this might be good for me. I tended to sleep late on Saturdays, so I hoped this task would force me to get up early and after delivering the papers I could use the time for my graduate work. So I agreed. I started delivering papers with Jason with the attitude that I was just fulfilling my obligations as a father. As time went on I was surprised to discover that I enjoyed it. It became a kind of ritual. Father and son developed an efficient plan for delivering papers. Father and son loaded the bundles of papers into our car. Father and son delivered them in less than an hour. Jason kept track of how much time it took and constantly looked for ways to shave a few more minutes off our delivery time. It was a very private game. Only two could play.

After the papers were delivered, father and son would go out for breakfast. McDonald's was always Jason's preferred place. Jason was supposed to buy my breakfast in return for my help, but most of the time I just ordered a cup of coffee. I didn't want to "eat" his profits, but on some of those achingly cold winter mornings I would order hotcakes. Jason didn't care, and he always ordered a big breakfast. I know he liked our Saturday breakfasts together; he even liked paying for dad's meal. I liked these breakfasts too, but my real "reward" was not the food.

Jason and I delivered more than papers on those Saturday mornings; we gave something to each other. In part it was simply the shared experience. At other times it was more of an adventure as we battled freezing temperatures or snow drifts as high as the car. On those mornings both of us felt a special sense of accomplishment. More than anything it was a time to be together, just the two of us, father and son. We developed a quiet intimacy. It was nothing we said. It was being cold together, stomping through snow drifts together, getting warm together, eating breakfast together. It was a time to say "I love you" without the words.

*   *   *

When Jason went to middle school, Jan and I had encouraged him to take extracurricular activities so that he would be identified with a group, but Jason didn't want to do this. When he began to have trouble with some of the other boys, we reminded him that his lack of involvement with any group outside of the classroom contributed to the problem. He perceived high school as a chance to make a fresh start, and he immediately signed up for marching band. He played percussion. During the first few months of his freshman year, another drummer began to harass him verbally. When Jason didn't respond the boy began to hit him with drumsticks, always being careful to do so when the band director wasn't looking. This was not particularly painful, but Jason was furious. He had had enough of such treatment.

Jason could have come home complaining, blaming us for bad advice, but he didn't. In fact, Jason did not even mention the situation. He was in high school now, and he wanted to solve this problem himself. He just wasn't sure how to do it. He finally talked to a school counselor who suggested that he keep a written record of everything the boy did to him. When he had enough evidence, he could show his notes to the band director. Jason liked the idea, and began keeping careful notes. He probably had enough documentation after a week or two, but he endured the harassment for over a month because he wanted overwhelming evidence.

When Jason decided his notes were copious enough, he presented them to the band director who could hardly believe what he read. He was amazed by Jason's patience in waiting so long before bringing the notes to him. The other boy's parents were asked to come to school with their son and they were confronted with the evidence. The boy confessed and was reprimanded. Although he was allowed to remain in the band, the boy continued to cause other problems and the director eventually expelled him. When Jason finally told me what had happened, I was a little worried that the boy might try to get even by attacking Jason after school, but he never did. He never bothered Jason again, and Jason took immense satisfaction from this successful strategy. He had solved the problem that had plagued him since fourth grade. He had found a nonviolent way to respond to bullying. You could almost see his sense of self-confidence rise. It was another of those small but important triumphs.

*   *   *

When sorting through Jason's papers after the accident, I found two letters he had written to a high school girl. Jason met her while working at Taco John's. I had talked to her briefly at the visitation and after the funeral. She and Jason had written some poetry together. After hearing of Jason's death, she wrote him a letter to say goodbye and gave it to me to put in the coffin. The two letters I found had been written last year while Jason was at college. The longer letter simply described what he was doing at the moment. In one paragraph he mentioned purchasing Garrison Keillor's latest book which he had begun to read. The shorter letter turned out to be a love letter. He not only wrote that he loved her, but that he wanted to marry her and he explained why she should accept his proposal.

To the best of my knowledge, Jason had not even had a date with her, so this "marriage proposal" was certainly a surprise. I suspected it would surprise the girl as well. They had become friends because they often worked the same shift. Most of Taco John's employees were high school students working part-time. They called themselves "taco buddies." The manager was a woman who was genuinely interested in her young staff and cared about them as people, not just as employees. She would organize parties for the "taco buddies" at Christmas and on other occasions. When she left Taco John's, they gave her a surprise farewell party. Jason had enjoyed the parties and the comraderie of the "taco buddies," but comraderie is not exactly an appropriate basis for a marriage proposal. I assumed that Jason had not expressed his feelings to her. Obviously, he had not mailed the letter.

I showed the letters to Jan. She thought it would be appropriate to give the longer letter to the girl, but we weren't sure what to do with the shorter one. Jason often wrote rough drafts of letters which he recopied before mailing. He would sometimes write letters and forget to mail them, but he also wrote letters which he never intended to mail. The fact that he wrote the love letter did not mean that he planned to mail it. As we talked, Jan and I began to see the love letter as simply an expression of the romantic side of Jason's personality. The letter was more like a valentine than a real marriage proposal. It was like carving initials on a park bench or sending flowers with a card from a "secret admirer." We decided to give both letters to the girl, but we wanted to do it in person so we could explain our perception of the love letter.

The girl's brother was also one of the "taco buddies," so I invited both of them to our house. When they came, we sat in the living room and talked for a while. Finally I brought out Jason's letters and gave them to the girl. I said I had found the letters among Jason's things, and that I assumed Jason had never mailed them, but I thought she should have them. The girl glanced at the shorter letter and it didn't take long to realize what it said. I could see the look of surprise and confusion. I immediately assured her that I understood that Jason's feelings for her were much stronger than her feelings for him. This did not matter. What was important was that he had experienced such a feeling during his lifetime.

Loving someone enough to think of marrying her is one of the finest feelings a man can have, and I explained to her how good it made me feel to know that Jason had felt and expressed such an emotion before his death. The love letter was also important because of the advice it contained. I asked her to look at one paragraph in particular. Jason had written that love meant looking past a person's physical appearance to measure the depth of his character and his commitment to relationship. He advised her to marry someone who would both appreciate her and encourage her, someone who would help her to achieve her goals rather than a man who demanded her full attention to his needs and his goals. Even though that person could not be Jason, it was still good advice. I asked her to think of it as a parting gift and to read both letters in that spirit. She seemed a little embarrassed, and perhaps a little pleased as well. I hope so. She was obviously special to Jason. I wanted her to know that, and to take some joy from that.

*   *   *

If I were to describe my son to a stranger, I would need a photograph I do not have. It would show Jason going in or out of a movie theater. I have no single anecdote to accompany the image. To describe his passion for film and filmmaking, I can only relate incidents and conversations which, in combination, might suggest how important films were to him.

When I took Jason to "Star Wars" he fell in love with it. Initially he was fascinated with the spectacle—the sights and sounds of a different world. As he got older, the passion intensified. If Jason liked a film, he saw it more than once. If he loved a film, he saw it several times. He had "Star Wars" on videotape and would boast that he had seen the film over a hundred times. Although Jason was capable of exaggeration, I am certain that this was the truth.

During middle school Jason seemed to use movies as an escape. The "real world" wasn't always pleasant but in the theater he could forget about that. In the theater the lights would go down and Jason would clutch his coke and popcorn in anticipation of the pleasure to be provided to all his senses. He would go with friends or alone; it didn't matter. For me, the main pleasure of seeing a film with friends is to talk about the film afterwards, but Jason didn't much care for this at first. Talking about films seemed to spoil them.

Jason was often a minimalist in the art of conversation during adolescence. If he answered the phone when friends or colleagues called, they would be treated to his crisp one or two word responses. Some people joked about my "Clint Eastwood answering service." When Jason first mentioned becoming a film major at the University of Iowa, I couldn't resist teasing him about having a major in the Department of Communication Studies, but he didn't appreciate my humor. He emphasized that his interest was in *visual* communication, not verbal. He wanted to create images, explore new worlds. He presented an impassioned and eloquent argument. His point was well taken and I apologized for my comment, and I was secretly pleased to have witnessed this demonstration of his verbal skills. He obviously had them when he chose to use them.

Jason and Matt spent a lot of time discussing films, but it took time before Jason would do so with me. He knew I had strong opinions, and I suspect he waited until he thought he could "hold his own" in a discussion with me. I remember one conversation during his senior in high school. We had both recently seen "Dead Poets Society," and although I liked the movie I did not believe that the young man's motivation for committing suicide was convincing. Jason agreed that the character of the authoritarian father was not fully developed, but he argued that it was developed enough to lend credibility to the young man's decision to kill himself. Although we could not agree on this point, it was a lively debate and I think Jason felt a sense of the pleasure I always found in discussing movies.

Jason's love affair with films affected almost everything he did. Jan had suggested taking a family trip that summer before Jason left for college. We discussed several possibilities, but Jason was to make the final decision. He picked Chicago. We went to a Cub's game, and of course, the Hard Rock Cafe, but the highlights of the trip for Jason had to do with movies. For example, I was surprised when Jason said he wanted to go to the Art Institute because he had not expressed much interest in art before. During our visit to the Institute, I understood the reason for his interest. He spent his time looking for particular paintings which had appeared in the film "Ferris Bueller's Day Off." Jason also wanted to photograph the front of the Art Institute, the Federal Building, Union Station, and other locations which were used in filming either "Ferris Bueller" or "The Untouchables." While taking photographs, Jason described scenes that were filmed at each location, even some of the camera angles. He took dozens of photographs.

Another highlight of the Chicago trip for Jason was not planned. The Science Institute happened to have a travelling exhibit concerning special effects in movies. We had to go, of course, and Jason thoroughly enjoyed it. At the same time, I was impressed with how much he already knew about the topic. Certain special effects experts were featured in the exhibit and Jason described some of the films these experts had worked on and he explained certain effects for which they were best known. His familiarity with their work made it apparent that he was not simply mindlessly watching the films which he rented over and over.

Over and over. So much that limits had to be imposed. Jan had purchased a membership and a credit account at a local movie rental outlet. At one point we had to tell them not to let Jason use our account to rent films. If he wanted a film he had to pay for it himself. Even so, he still found ways for us to support his "habit." Once I tried to rent a film and charge it to my account but they would not let me rent the film until I paid the late fee for my last rental. I had no idea what they were talking about. They said their records showed that I had rented a Spencer Tracy film entitled "A Guy Named Joe." I immediately assumed that Jason had something to do with this, but I had never heard of the film and I could not imagine why Jason would want to see it. Later I read that Steven Spielberg was working on a remake of an old Spencer Tracy film. Obviously, Jason had been doing his homework in preparation for seeing Spielberg's "Always." The film was completed in time for a Christmas release in 1989. Jason never got to see it.

Shortly after we returned from Europe, Jason asked Jan and me to come into the kitchen so he could explain and demonstrate a project he had completed while we were gone. He had bought some cable to connect the television sets in the living room and kitchen. He dropped the cable into the basement from the living room and strung it along the ceiling of the basement creating a maze of black spaghetti. Using a system of splitters and connectors, he brought the cable up into the kitchen. Now, anyone watching a movie on videotape in the living room could also watch it in the kitchen simply by flipping a switch near the television in the kitchen. Jason was quite proud of his work. I complimented him on his cleverness, but I couldn't suppress a smile as I asked if he was simply trying to avoid interruptions in his movie watching caused by wanting food or something to drink from the kitchen. Jason just smiled back at me.

When I am watching films on videotape now, I usually have both television sets turned on so I can wander from one room to the next just as Jason would have done. I have been renting films more often since Jason's death. In the past movies did not represent an "escape" for me. I used to demand that a movie teach me something, offer a new insight, provide a different perspective. Now I enjoy a film that simply makes me feel good. I like to pretend that Jason is next to me, enjoying the film with me. And we don't have to talk about it afterwards.

CHAPTER 7
Surviving

... that mortal man who hath more of joy than sorrow in him, that mortal man cannot be true—not true, or undeveloped. With books the same. The truest of all men was the Man of Sorrows ... and Ecclesiastes is the fine hammered steel of woe . . . There is a wisdom that is woe; but there is a woe that is madness. [15, pp. 542-543]

Herman Melville
Moby Dick

The newspaper obituaries always conclude with the statement that the deceased "is survived by" (mother, father, spouse, daughter, son). For the first time in my adult life I was identified as a survivor, and the word began to have new meaning for me. I felt like a survivor. I felt like someone who had been sailing through peaceful waters when suddenly the vessel had smashed into unseen and treacherous rocks. I found myself on a grim and forbidding shore, staring at my wife and daughter, looking desperately for my son, beginning to understand that I was not going to find him, that he did not "make it." There is an old riddle that asks "Where did they bury the survivors?" I had an answer now that had nothing to do with the riddle, but everything to do with what it means to be a survivor.

Surviving means to go on living when a part of you has died. Surviving means going to work and smiling at people and doing the things you have always done, and being the only one who knows that you are only pretending to be what you were. Surviving means going to movies and crying easily, sometimes when everyone else is laughing. When "The Little Mermaid" came to town I took Tess to see it. There was one romantic scene where the prince and the mermaid are sitting in a rowboat while animated animals surround them singing a lively song called "Kiss the Girl." I knew how much Jason would have enjoyed this scene and tears flowed down my face.

Surviving means seeing the "sermon in every stone" advocated by the Puritans. One evening I was sitting in the living room when I noticed that one of the two lights above the fireplace had burnt out, leaving a corner of the room in darkness. I thought of my children. My daughter still cast her bright light but my son's death had darkened a corner of my world. One December evening the living room was dark except for the lights on the Christmas tree. When one string of lights suddenly blinked out, the Christmas tree seemed to symbolize my family tree, and life seemed a struggle between light and darkness. If life was a celebration lighting up the darkness, then death was a shadow. The struggle was futile. As the shadow lengthened, darkness dimmed the lights, until all were extinguished. Such are the musings of a survivor.

Just before Christmas a woman from Steven Spielberg's film company called and left a message apologizing for being so slow in responding to my letter. She explained that they had been busy finishing "Always," Spielberg's latest film scheduled for a Christmas release. The woman sounded genuinely sorry and said we would soon be receiving something. I was surprised by her apology, but I appreciated her sensitivity and concern. A few days later a cardboard tube came in the mail. It contained a poster signed by Spielberg. No instructions came with it so Jan and I decided to frame it and put it in the guest room next to the photographs of the Lucas poster. We thought of it as a Christmas present for Jason. He would have been thrilled.

Christmas. People had advised us to travel during Christmas because the holidays can be the hardest time. After our European trip last summer, Jan and Tess and I had each qualified for a free ticket on our frequent flyer cards. Before Jason's accident we had talked about using those tickets to fly to California for Christmas. One of my sisters lived in a Los Angeles suburb and a nephew lived in San Diego. Jason had wanted to go with us. I wondered if we would be able to enjoy the trip now. Several friends insisted that it would be the best thing to do, so we went.

It was a good decision, even though it didn't stop me from thinking about Jason. In fact, I thought of Jason often during the trip. I wondered if he would have enjoyed the football game at the Holiday Bowl. He was not a sports fan, but he appreciated a good spectacle. I know he would have liked our short shopping spree in Tijuana, but he would have been especially excited about staying at the Hotel del

Coronado. I could imagine him strolling through its majestic lobby and explaining its place in the history of filmmaking (amply documented in various photographs on the walls of the halls leading to the lobby).

The most bittersweet time for me was during the tour of Universal Studios. Jason would have been impressed with everything that had been added since we had been there nine years ago. At one point in the guided tour I spotted a bungalow with a sign in front partially hidden by shrubbery but I could see this much:

mblin'
tertainment

Although the tour guide said nothing, I knew "Amblin' Entertainment" was the name of Steven Spielberg's production company. If only Jason could have been there! I would have pointed out the sign and it would have been one of the highlights of the tour for him. I could imagine him telling his friends about it. I could imagine him conveniently forgetting to mention that Dad saw it first. (And I would have smiled and let him take the credit.)

Jason always enjoyed buying souvenirs, and there were many shops with sweatshirts and caps and movie mementoes. I found a picture frame in the shape of a "take board" which I had to buy because I knew Jason would have wanted it. He would have wanted many of the items. He probably would have spent most of his own money and then lobbied with Jan to buy more and she would have, although not enough to satisfy him. I could imagine their dialogue clearly (having heard it so often on previous trips) that it seemed as though it had happened, and I had to remind myself that it didn't happen. Jason wasn't here.

This experience reminded me of a scene I had witnessed as a teenager while riding with my father in his rendering works truck. We had driven to a pasture where we were supposed to pick up a dead calf. The cattle were clustered in groups. My father drove toward a cow standing alone near her calf and licking it. The mother was doing all that she could to comfort the calf, to heal it, to make it well, but the calf was dead. The calf looked pretty small, so my father asked me to help him pick it up. This would save some time. When we drove up next to the calf, the mother moved away, but not far away. She watched as my father let down the rear gate of the truck; she watched as my father and I grabbed her calf by the legs and threw it into the truck; she watched as my father and I closed and locked the rear gate.

My father had to turn around and drive out the way we came, so I rolled down my window and watched the mother slowly walk back to where her calf had been. She sniffed the empty spot, then looked up at the departing truck. She began to run. At first I thought she was running after the truck, but she was running in a circle around the calfless spot. She ran in ever widening circles while we drove out of the pasture and she was still running when we reached the road and drove away. I have been told that animals are incapable of feeling emotion, but I'm not so sure this is true. The image of that animal running in circles has surfaced at times as my mind races around the empty places Jason once occupied. That is also what it means to be a survivor.

When we returned from California I went to the cemetery right away. I wanted to be certain no one had tampered with Jason's Christmas tree, decorated with rolls of film, Oscar statues and conventional ornaments. Jan had gone on a cold day and poured hot water to soften the ground so she could secure the tree by driving large nails through the holes in the tree stand. She worried that the wind might blow it away, and some tombstones had been vandalized in recent years.

When I went to the cemetery, the tiny Christmas tree stood undisturbed next to a wreath propped up against the monument. The green colors of the wreath and tree contrasted with the barren trees in the cemetery and the snow covered ground and the gray, overcast sky. As I looked more closely at the Christmas tree, I noticed a white ticket stub. One of Jason's friends must have gone to a movie before coming to visit Jason's grave and then stuck the ticket stub onto the end of the branch. I appreciated the sentiment. I began to think about Jason's friends. When you are nineteen, life is supposed to stretch out like an endless highway. Suddenly a friend is gone, and friends find themselves forced to be survivors too.

As I stood by Jason's grave, I was tempted to talk to him. I wanted to tell him about the trip to California, about the Christmas presents, especially the ring Jan and Tess had given me with rubies set in it. The ruby was Jason's birthstone. Jason loved Christmas, and I wanted to tell him about it, about the gifts and the dinner, so I did. I also talked about Garrison Keillor's offer to do a benefit for his scholarship fund. I talked about my writing, how I was trying to express my joy in having him for a son, and my sorrow in losing him so soon. I said I had written enough for a small book; perhaps it could become a book someday. I smiled as I suggested that Spielberg could make a movie from it. "Who would you want to play you Jason?" And then my eyes filled up with tears and I could not stop from weeping.

Since dreams were the only opportunity for "seeing" Jason, I went to bed every night hoping to dream about him, promising myself not to try to touch him or hug him this time so that the dream would last longer, but I did not dream of him. My dreams resumed the pattern that had existed before the "bridge" dream—mundane extensions of the day's events or those occasional nightmares stemming from common human fears and anxieties. Only once did I dream of Jason again, but that was in the early morning and I was partly conscious. I'm not certain if it was really a dream or if the image I saw was shaped by my conscious desire to dream of Jason.

This "dream" had no plot. I simply saw Jason and, despite my earlier resolution, went to hug him. I could not stop myself. Jason's face was expressionless, although I thought I detected a certain repugnance. Was it for tolerating my hug? Was it for being forced back into his body, a body of which he was always self-conscious when he was alive? I don't know, but he didn't disappear this time. He was slightly above me. When I hugged him my head was pressed to his chest, but I could hear no heartbeat, nor the sound of breathing. Although he seemed to be alive, it was so quiet inside his body. It did not feel heavy like the body at the funeral home nor cold like the body in the hospital. Jason said nothing and did not return my hug. And then I was wide awake. It was not a satisfying dream. I have not dreamed of Jason again.

I continued to go to the cemetery on a regular basis, but except for that time after the Christmas trip, I have had little to say. Jan has also visited the cemetery regularly, and we have discussed our need to do that. Jan sometimes talks when she's there, even though she does not "feel" Jason's presence. She talks because talking seems to help. I usually do not talk. I simply stare at the words on the monument and think of Jason's dreams, or I squat in front of the stone and trace the letters of Jason's name with my finger. Once I said, "I love you Jason." It felt good to say, as if my heart was so full of these words they were ready to spill out. Since then I often say, just before I leave, "I love you Jason. I miss you."

In February, the people in charge of the arrangements for the Keillor benefit scheduled a press conference. It was to be the official announcement concerning the benefit for Jason's scholarship fund. My task was to explain why I wrote the letters and to describe my reaction to Keillor's offer to do this benefit. Just before I was to speak, a press release was read which provided the context for this event. It stated in a dispassionate, journalistic manner that Jason was "killed" when he was "19 years old," a "tragic death." Although I had been thinking of

Jason's death constantly, I had not heard those words spoken aloud since the accident. The words struck me like a fist hammering against my chest. My heart was pounding and my legs were quivering by the time I reached the microphones. I was almost unable to speak.

My voice trembled as I began. I stopped to drink some water and tried to continue but my voice still trembled and the words came out in spurts. I paused and took a deep breath and tried to resume, but the tears flowed faster than words. The words were not necessary; it became obvious why I wrote the letters. I was in pain and didn't know what else to do. Words are the tools of my trade. I read; I write; I listen; I respond. I sent the letters out like flares in the darkness of my despair pleading "Here I am, over here, help me."

Jan walked to the microphones and stood beside me as I managed to reach the point where Keillor called from New York. I stepped aside and let Jan finish the narration. I walked away from the lights and cameras and microphones and tried to "collect" myself. It is an apt phrase. I felt fragmented, and I was not certain where all the pieces were. At the same time I felt miserable, as though I had performed poorly at an audition. This feeling quickly gave way to anger:

> Who gave me the role of the grieving father?
> Don't people have the right to choose the roles they are supposed to
> play?
> Why wasn't I asked if I wanted this part?
> I don't.

It was unseasonably warm that February and all the snow had melted. Winter without snow is a depressing experience. The snow conceals the dead vegetation and should not disappear until the spring thaw which transforms the earth into the mud and slime from which new life will emerge in this annual rite of renewal. As spring approached now, there was no snow to disguise the earth. The ground was exposed, revealing the frozen, brown and barren look of winter. There was no hint of green. It was difficult to believe in Spring's promise of rebirth.

The week before the Keillor benefit was hectic as Jan and I prepared for all the friends and family who would be coming. On Friday we went to the high school to draw the winning raffle ticket for the Lucas poster. Before the drawing, it was announced that the raffle had raised $600 for the scholarship fund. When the number was drawn, it belonged to a shy young woman who had purchased a ticket at the last minute. She seemed surprised and embarrassed by her good fortune. Jan and I stood at her side with the poster in front of us as our picture was taken.

Most of our family and friends began arriving on Friday. On Saturday evening, several members of the Koppelman family went to a restaurant for a quiet celebration of my parents' fiftieth wedding anniversary. My mother and father had insisted on having nothing more than dinner, but Jan and I had a surprise party at our house with champagne, an anniversary cake, and a few gifts. Everyone enjoyed themselves. It was good to have something to celebrate.

On Sunday morning, Keillor and some friends drove down from Minneapolis in a van. Jan and Tess and I went to the theatre after Keillor had arrived and were introduced to him. I gave him a scrapbook containing photographs of Jason, the last poem Jason had written, press clippings about the benefit, and a copy of a letter Jason had written in which he explained why he liked Keillor's book. Keillor was gracious and distant at the same time. He was involved in the preparations for the performance and was in the midst of conducting a "sound check" when we arrived. After a brief conversation, I thanked him for coming and stood off to the side to watch the preparations. A reporter from a Milwaukee newspaper asked if Jan and I would grant him an interview, so we went into the corridor to talk with him.

When we returned to the stage, Keillor was singing a verse from a gospel song, "His eye is on the sparrow, and I know He's watching me" [16]. My heart beat faster at the coincidence of Keillor singing a song based on the biblical passage which I had so closely associated with Jason's death. I wondered if he planned to sing the song during the show. It had been a long time since I heard the song so I could not remember the words, but I could already feel the tears welling up.

Despite my efforts to remain calm, powerful and conflicting emotions surged inside me. I was thrilled to meet Keillor whose work I had enjoyed for so long, but my delight was curbed by the thought that this event was due to Jason's death. It was gratifying to see all the people coming to the benefit, but the one person I wanted most to see could not be there. I reminded myself that the money generated by this performance would make it possible to offer scholarships from the Jason David Koppelman fund by next spring, but I knew how inadequately this would fill the void caused by Jason's death. The attention from the press and the momentary notoriety were exciting, but the one who would have enjoyed it most was dead. Andy Warhol said that in the future everyone would become a celebrity for fifteen minutes. He did not say that such status might be posthumous for some. He did not say how unwanted or unsatisfying it could be.

When the "sound check" was concluded, I approached Keillor once again to mention that Jan and I wanted to take him to see Jason's grave after the benefit. We wanted him to see the words we had borrowed from him for the monument. He graciously accepted our invitation. Since the cemetery was not far away, I knew we would have enough time to go there and return for the start of the reception scheduled to follow the benefit. Now that all the preparations were concluded, Keillor left to be alone for the final thirty minutes before the show began.

People were coming. I recognized some of the faces but not many. Tess was talking to one of her friends and Jan had gone to the room scheduled for the reception to assist with the preparations. I did not feel like talking to anyone, but I did not know what else to do. I decided to take my seat in the theatre so that I could sit quietly and think. My seat was in the middle of a block of seats which had been purchased for family and friends, including Jason's friends. I was the only one sitting in this block of seats for ten minutes or more until family members began arriving.

The theatre filled quickly. Additional seats had been set up onstage which created an intimate atmosphere. A friend whom I had not seen for almost ten years was coming, and I worried whether he would be able to find the theatre from my directions. When I saw him walking down the aisle with his daughter, I was so happy to see him I walked down the row, stepping carefully around everyone's feet, until I reached him and we hugged. I thanked him for coming. As I returned to my seat, Keillor and his pianist walked on stage and were greeted with enthusiastic applause.

It was a special occasion for me from the moment Keillor began. It was a performance filled with sentiment and humor, with warmth and compassion. He sang the opening song acappella. The "country and western" melody was intended to reinforce his pun on writer/rider:

Well, I come from the prairie, but I live in New York—
A tall, lonesome cowboy and slightly historic,
But I am a writer, I write every day
On my big Underwood 'cross the wide open page.

I write in the morning and I write at night;
I've written with Thurber, Mark Twain, E.B. White.
They mostly write better than I and I mean it,
But I am still livin' and that is convenient.

The song set the stage for the entire performance which was a celebration of life, with pauses to consider such perplexing questions as why those of us fortunate enough to be alive are given this privilege? Although he could provide no answer, Keillor expressed a humble gratitude for the opportunity. The music was part of the celebration, but the atmosphere was largely created by the language of a master storyteller.

Keillor gently reminded the audience that we don't always appreciate the gift of life. To illustrate the folly of such ingratitude, he paraphrased the philosophy of the "Sons of Knute" from Lake Wobegon:

Some luck lies not in getting what you think you want, but getting what you have, which, once you have it, you may be lucky enough to see is what you would've wanted had you known . . . It's a complicated philosophy.

Part of the reason Keillor's stories are so effective in engaging an audience is that the storyteller himself does not pretend to be immune to human weakness:

Anyone who has ever done comedy on stage, deep down in their hearts their secret desire is to sing. You always want something else, you know.

I appreciated the self deprecating humor because of my own antagonism to the accolades heaped on the "self-made man" and the "rugged individualist." C. Wright Mills once claimed that the people promoting such ideas are most often those who have inherited their father's farm or factory. Such notions have caused Americans to forget the need to be humble, to be gracious, to appreciate the gifts and rewards we are given in life:

I always like to tell jokes, and as long as people laugh it's good, and then if they don't laugh so much I call it humor. It's not comedy any more. And then when they don't laugh at all I like to sing, and then they laugh again and I become a comedian. So you see, it just goes in a circle.

Of course the part I appreciated most was when Keillor sat on a stool and talked about the reason for this benefit, to raise money for a scholarship fund in memory of:

> . . . a reader of mine, Jason David Koppelman. A person doesn't get all that many readers, you know, and you hate to see one go. So I came out here in memory of this lovely young man, so funny and lively, but of course, he was a reader of mine, so of course he was. I got a chance to look at a letter he wrote; I looked at it today. He wrote this not long before he died, and (he wrote) about this book of mine which he actually bought with his own money. What an amazing honor to be paid that a kid would shell out all that money . . . and then he would make phone calls, his dad tells me, to his friends and read them parts of my book at long distance rates! I really feel honored by that. One of his favorite parts of it was a little poem in the front:

> My parents think I'm crazy,

> My kids think I'm bourgeois

> (*Keillor paused to note*—"*He didn't have any kids, but he had an imagination.*")

> My true love thinks I'm wonderful,

> The handsomest she ever saw,

> And who am I to disagree

> With one so sensible as she?

Although this was one of only a few direct references to Jason in the show, there was much in the performance to remind me of Jason. Keillor talked of growing up in the midwest, of coping with shyness, of being fascinated with girls, of being preoccupied with romantic fantasies, of wishing to escape from parental supervision. It was pure fabrication; it was absolute truth. It was about all adolescents; it was about certain adolescents; it was about Jason. Keillor described a childhood memory of an aunt who made wonderful lemon meringue pies. As he closed his eyes he seemed to be savoring the smell of "the sharpness of the lemon and the sweetness of the sugar." The dialogue which follows was his recreation of himself as a young boy requesting a piece of that heavenly smelling pie. His aunt responds:

> "It's always better if you wait. You can wait until this evening, can't you?"
> "But what if the Lord came this afternoon . . . and took us all up to heaven. I'd never get to taste it then."
> "But there would be better things than lemon meringue pie in heaven."
> "Perhaps, but how can anything be better than perfection? It would be a shame to be up there and not to have tasted everything that you could taste."

Jason shared such a view of life, and he would have smiled at that story. The more Keillor talked, the more I understood why Jason enjoyed his books and tapes so much. They had much in common, from the conventional experience of sibling rivalry to the problem of being too shy and insecure to ask a girl for a date. Another similarity emerged when Keillor noted the absurdity of his parents punishing him by sending him up to his room, whereas the real punishment would have been to send him out to play with other kids. Like Keillor, Jason had always enjoyed being alone. Perhaps the most personal similarity between them became obvious when Keillor discussed the reasons why he became a radio performer. He described his perception of the "magic" of radio:

> It had always been my dream, since I was a kid, to be invisible . . . to be able to talk to people and say what you want to say to them without having to endure them looking at you as you say it.

Jason would have understood. He wanted to major in film and become a director because of the "magic" of movies. He didn't want to be a part of the images, but he wanted to create images for others to see. He wanted to create a world for people to enjoy, if only temporarily. Jason was determined to achieve this dream. Keillor quoted Henry David Thoreau, "If we advance confidently in the direction of our dreams, we will accomplish a success we could not have dreamed of in our waking hours." Jason believed in his dreams. He was confident that he would achieve them.

At the conclusion of the performance, Keillor repeated how honored he felt to do this benefit for the scholarship fund "in memory of my reader," and said he wanted to end it by reading from "an essay that he liked." Keillor read the essay "Laying on Our Backs Looking Up at the

Stars" and the audience listened to a midwestern celebration of life, of good friends, of being a parent, of just being [5]. When Keillor finished reading he closed the book. After the applause began to diminish Keillor said that he had borrowed this copy of his book from his son who was born the same year as Jason and was also named Jason. As he casually thumbed through the pages of the book he said, "It doesn't look as if he's read this." Keillor smiled and the audience laughed, but I recognized the bittersweet voice of the parent.

All parents want their children to understand life as they perceive it because this is essential for the children to be able to understand and accept their parents. Jason had many unpleasant experiences in his life, more than I had at his age, and I often wondered if it was even possible for him to share my belief in life's goodness and its opportunities for joy. The poetry Jason had written at college revealed the frustration and even alienation he was feeling, yet he could read Keillor's book, amid all his misery and loneliness, and recognize that this essay said something truthful about the goodness of life.

After the benefit, Jan and I made our way through the crowd and through a side door on the stage. Keillor was standing there with his coat on. None of us talked much on the way to the cemetery. Keillor was humming a tune at first, but then he was quiet. He did apologize for a story he told during the show which included a teenage driver having a car accident in which no one was hurt. It had not upset Jan or me and I said no apology was necessary. He explained that once he got started on a story he did not always know where it would take him.

At the cemetery we walked over to the monument and stared in silence for a moment. Keillor asked why we chose Jason for our son's name. We told him the story, and he responded with the reason he gave the same name to his son. As we began to walk back to the car, Keillor stopped to look back one more time at the side of the monument with the simplified version of "Starry Night" and the title of Keillor's essay carved across the top. He said there certainly wasn't another monument in the cemetery like this one. That was true.

On the way back the conversation continued to be sporadic and somewhat awkward. It finally dawned on me that Keillor is genuinely shy. Although I had heard him talk about this and read the essays where he claimed to be shy, it was difficult to believe because he is a performer. He had just given a masterful performance, but now he was with two strangers still grieving over the loss of their son. I should not have been surprised that he didn't know what to say. He didn't need to say much. He had done more than enough already.

At the reception Keillor was gracious and patient. He chatted with everyone. He signed pictures and books and programs, usually writing more than just his name. He posed for pictures and smiled and joked and behaved like everyone's favorite uncle at the family picnic. Time did not concern him. As people began to leave, I suggested that Keillor and his friends should follow me in their van to a restaurant. We had reserved a private room for supper.

By the time I arrived, most of the invited guests were already there. When Keillor entered the room a few minutes later, he noticed Jason's friends sitting at one table. He went over and told them not sit by themselves but to mingle with the others. He even picked up some dishes and silverware and arranged for them to sit at different tables around the room. Jason's friends looked both embarrassed and pleased. After supper Keillor and his friends entertained us by singing a few more songs. It was a continuation of the celebration of life begun at the benefit.

I was surprised that Keillor stayed so late. He was supposed to fly to New York the next day, so he and his friends would have to drive back to St. Paul that night. Jan came up and whispered her suggestion that I stand up and formally express our appreciation before Keillor and his friends had to leave. I had not thought about this, but it was obviously an appropriate thing to do. I wasn't certain what I wanted to say when I tapped on my water glass to get everyone's attention, but I decided to speak from the heart, letting my feelings dictate the words.

I began by saying that we like to think we have choices as we go through life, but occasionally something happens over which you have no control. This can create a sense of helplessness and even despair. At such times it is easy to forget that we still have choices. I thanked Garrison and his friends for choosing to come here and to perform in the benefit for Jason's scholarship fund. Their decision reminded me that even though I had to accept a sorrow I did not choose, I still had other choices. In addition to everything else this benefit meant for me and all of us, I was especially grateful to them for reminding me of that. I sat down. Everyone applauded while I tried to drink from a glass of water with a trembling hand. I realized how exhausted I was from the emotional upheaval of this day.

Some people began to move around; others sat; everyone talked. Keillor and his friends left and gradually so did everyone else. It was almost 10:00 when we came home. My parents were staying at our house, as was the friend whom I had not seen in almost ten years. His daughter went with Tess to her room and everyone else went to bed except for my friend and me. We stayed up and talked for five or six hours until fatigue forced us to bed.

All of our visitors left the next day. Jan and I had previously arranged to stay home from work on the day after the benefit. We knew we would be tired and would need some time to recuperate, but we had not anticipated how tired we would be. We did not leave the house for the entire day. I read the articles describing the benefit in the local newspaper, but I felt vaguely dissatisfied. Although the articles contained accurate descriptions of the benefit, the meaning of the event was missing. I didn't blame the reporters because what I wanted was not the kind of article journalists are supposed to write.

A few days later I read a letter to the editor about the benefit. It was written by Donald Fox, a minister who had just moved to town and served in a church near our house. He described the benefit in a way that clarified my reaction to it:

> . . . Keillor's show in memory of Jason Koppelman was a religious experience . . .
>
> The ancient Greeks were a religious people, yet their temples and their ritual worship failed to provide them with an outlet for expressing their religion intellectually. Worshiping at a distance a deity enclosed within a temple or watching a priest perform a ritual sacrifice and divination did not engage the emotions of people who loved to think, reason and laugh. And so the Greeks developed their great theater out of a religious need. The theater became a place where they worshiped as a community while engaging their hearts, mind and souls.
>
> Garrison Keillor provided those of us fortunate to be present with a modern example of the ancient Greek ideal of theater as a religious experience. In Kierkegaard's phrase, he performed "a work of love in remembering one dead." He touched our hearts and souls . . . The ancient Greeks gave us the word for what Mr. Keillor accomplished: catharsis.

This letter expressed for me the meaning of the benefit and the healing it provided. I was able to write a letter of thanks to Garrison Keillor because it was now possible for me to say what I needed to say. When I wrote to him, I returned to the question I was supposed to answer at the February press conference about why I had written the letters to Jason's heroes. I had thought that the reason primarily involved what I could do for Jason, or for his memory. I had thought I was merely asking his heroes to take note of his passing. I knew that writing the letters also had therapeutic value for me, but I was not quite honest in confronting that part of it. I had convinced myself that I was prepared to receive no responses, but now I understood more clearly the enormity of the pain which was the context for writing those letters.

I said earlier that I felt like a shipwrecked survivor cast ashore, but my metaphor was not accurate. I may have made it to shore, but I had gone back into the turbulent waters to find my son, swimming in circles like the cow circling the calfless space. It was a futile effort. When Keillor offered to do this benefit, it was like throwing me a life preserver, and I clutched it gratefully. He provided a new path or a different direction. I would have survived if he had not done this (I have learned how to be a survivor), but he made the transition easier.

The benefit represented another stage in the "rescue." It helped to draw me closer to my family, closer to the safety of shore. This is what I tried to explain when I wrote to thank Keillor for his kindness. I am still in turbulent waters because the suffering has not ceased, but these waters are not deep enough to be dangerous. It is up to me now, to continue the slow process of making my way back to shore.

PEOPLE

Keillor does show for fan

Garrison Keillor came to La Crosse, Wis., Sunday to do a show for a fan he never knew.

The fan, **Jason Koppelman**, was killed in a car accident last September. Koppelman, 19, a sophomore at Viterbo College in La Crosse, had loved Keillor's book "We Are Still Married." After his death, his parents, **Kent** and **Janet Koppelman**, wrote Keillor to tell him how he had enriched Jason's life.

Keillor was so moved by the letter that, about a week later, he called the Koppelmans and offered to do a show in La Crosse to raise money for the Jason Koppelman Scholarship Fund, established by the family to help La Crosse college students majoring in film or mass communication, Jason's fields of interest.

"It was completely initiated by him. I was just absolutely astounded," Janet Koppelman said Monday of Keillor's offer. "The fact that he has a son about (Jason's) age moved him."

On Sunday, Keillor performed for a packed theater of about 1,200 at Viterbo College, saying he was honored to perform for Jason's scholarship fund. "A person doesn't get all that many readers. You hate to see a good one go," he said.

The show raised about $25,000, boosting the fund to about $30,000. The first scholarship probably will be awarded next year, Janet Koppelman said.

Afterward, Keillor went with the Koppelmans to visit Jason's grave, and then attended a reception and dinner before leaving for St. Paul. "He was so thoughtful about everything," Janet Koppelman said. "I just can't say enough nice things about him."

Remembering the Dream:
A Self Portrait

Isn't It Romantic

I. It Could Happen to You
     . . . and we danced.
   The music poured into the air
   from a piano across the room
   and filled my soul with happiness
        and joy,
      as did the young woman in my arms.
   I've enjoyed her company for some
        time now.
   I am truly in love.
   as I hope she is with me
   Life cannot be better.

II. You Are Too Beautiful
        . . . and we danced.
      Every song seems to play slower
      and we are drawn closer.
      I flow in her presence.
      She rests her chin on my shoulder.
      The delicately soft fuzz of her face
           tingles
      as she nestles her cheek on my neck.
      The strands of her hair brush lightly
           on my face.
      One hand presses gently against her
           back
      as the other is suspended in air,
      with hers, in her warm grasp.
      She feels so fragile,
      yet I hold her tight for fear of losing
           her.

III. Isn't it Romantic

> . . . and we danced.
> Nothing has ever been more right.
> I raise my hand and lift up her head
> with a finger under her chin.
> "You *are* beauty," I say.
> She blushes and tries to look away.
> "I love you," I say.
> She turns back
> and stares into my eyes.
> I have never felt so free
> until . . .
> "I love you, too."
> I fall limp into her arms and cry.
> I've waited so long to hear that
> and now I *am* happiness and joy.
> . . . and we danced.

— Jason David Koppelman
(Summer – 1989)

CHAPTER 8
Asking

All mankind is of one author, and is one volume; when one man dies, one chapter is not torn out of the book, but translated into a better language; and every chapter must be so translated. [17, p. 340]

John Donne
"Meditation 17"

As grateful as I was to Garrison Keillor, I was troubled by one recurring thought—why should I receive any special treatment? Other parents have lost a son or a daughter and they hurt; they suffer. They get no special recognition; no celebrity comes to ease their pain.

Keillor wrote about this point of view in an essay aptly titled, "Who Do You Think You Are." It is not a question but an assertion—"You're no better than the rest of us." I have acted on that belief all my life; it is perhaps a peculiarly midwestern form of egalitarianism, but it has served me well. I have never respected (and cannot understand) the arrogance of those who think they should be accorded special treatment because of the money they have made or the status they have achieved (or were granted at birth). We are all food for worms. That should be a universal basis of humility.

I think Americans used to know that, but we have now sanitized death in so many ways that it does not seem real. There is a poem that used to be commonly found on American tombstones:

> Stranger, pause as you pass by,
> As you are now so once was I,
> As I am now so you shall be,
> Prepare for death and follow me.

151

Prepare for death. How is that done? Perhaps we should enjoy each day as it comes, make life a celebration of family and friends, appreciate the joy and pleasure of life, help others to appreciate life's possibilities, have compassion for others because we share a common destiny. This is a secular approach. For a believer (in any religion), the preparation for death would probably be similar, but would include additional commitments. It is my understanding that every major world religion expresses some concern for helping the poor, the needy, the less fortunate. This concern is related to preparation for death since most of those religions have some belief in a life after death where one is elevated to a higher consciousness based on how one has fulfilled the moral precepts of the religion. Whether it is called nirvana or heaven, most religions promise eternal life usually in the presence of a divine being.

From my observations of Christians today, there is little to suggest that preparing for death is of much concern. Instead, I have seen a curious pattern of behavior including denouncing welfare recipients (fast becoming our national pastime), complaining about the homeless, and refusing to hear the sounds of human suffering (animal suffering is another matter). The exceptions merely emphasize the pattern. This would appear to contradict what Jesus told his followers concerning those who are poor or homeless or hungry. If Christians want their taxes spent on defense (presumably to protect their worldly goods) rather than used to help alleviate suffering, how are they preparing for death according to Christian principles? The American principle seems to be "get the most for your money" based upon the belief that "you only go around once in life." If this is the dominant philosophy in our country for believers or nonbelievers alike, then it is a solipsistic version of preparing for death. It may have to do with the pursuit of happiness, but it has little to do with the experience of joy.

We all have to die. We have no choice about that. The choices we can make have to do with how we are going to live. What I am still feeling helplessly angry about is why my son had to die at nineteen in a car accident. Questions keep hounding me, demanding answers. Why couldn't he have been thrown from the car earlier? Why couldn't the car have rolled instead of tumbling onto its top? Why wasn't he given a chance to learn from whatever mistake he made which caused him to go off the road? When the tumult of such questions subsides, I am forced to face the reality that good people die every day—mothers, fathers, sons and daughters. Airplanes crash, cars smash, school walls collapse, flood and famine and disease all sweep their bloody scythe on the just and unjust alike.

There is only one question I have the power to answer—how do I go on? Some cultures have rituals to ease the pain of death, elaborate or simple rites to provide hope or bring peace to the bereaved. All we have are the visitations and a funeral. I can attest to their inadequacy. Much of what I have done since Jason's accident has been an attempt to invent a grieving process. Others have not been given as much help as I have. Not only was I offered sympathy, but the money raised by Garrison Keillor has established a scholarship fund to perpetuate Jason's memory. The realization that this is more than most survivors can expect has not comforted me. If anything, it has added to my discomfort. "You're no better than the rest of us." And so I come back to my original question, Why should I receive special treatment?

I began to be ashamed of the attention I had received, and that caused me to question those earlier events which had offered some consolation. I wondered if the door bursting open at the funeral was just a consequence of sporadic breezes, or if there was some other scientific explanation. After all, no one knew if the door had been closed tight. Jan finding Jason's glasses in the ditch could have been a matter of luck requiring no external assistance. Her sense of being told to look down could have stemmed from her increased vulnerability and her need to believe that Jason was still with us in some way. The dream of Jason after my prayer which gave me the energy to function more effectively could also have been a coincidence.

As time passed, my doubts grew stronger. It became increasingly difficult to believe that these events represented the intervention of a compassionate God. I was also frustrated by these doubts because they seemed so predictable, the consequence of a relentless attitude of "What have you done for me today?" It reminded me of the Israelites escaping from Egypt. The Exodus account described such extraordinary miracles as the parting of the Red Sea and manna falling from heaven, and when I was young I had difficulty believing that the Israelites could suddenly forget such extraordinary events and worship a golden calf. It seemed impossible to me that they could disown their faith so easily when they had witnessed such miraculous examples of divine intervention which literally preserved their lives. Now I understood how this could happen.

It was not about forgetting. Extraordinary events provoke powerful emotions which shape the perception of those events at the time they occur. When the emotions inevitably fade, so does the certainty about the meaning of the event. I am not suggesting that my experience was comparable to the Israelites, but it was analogous. When you witness an extraordinary event, an inner voice, intuition perhaps, interprets the experience so compellingly that you are convinced the interpretation is true, but as time passes there comes a cacophony of conflicting voices and your sense of certainty is shaken. You doubt the intuitive voice. If you regard yourself as a rational person, your rationality insists on a rational explanation. The Israelites were wandering in the desert and desperately needed to believe, to know they worshipped a God who would protect them. When they felt abandoned by Yahweh they made another god out of gold. Perhaps I worship at the shrine of reason. Perhaps that is my golden calf.

Part of my growing doubt stemmed from my egalitarianism. Who was I to think that God should pay such attention to me? Why should I deserve anything more than any other parent who loses a child? Jan never perceived a divine source for these events, but believed it was Jason trying to comfort us. I wondered if other parents had similar experiences but did not talk about them? People may not want to talk about such experiences for fear of accusations that they are being irrational or superstitious, or even that they are promoting a belief in the occult. Perhaps it has been a conspiracy of silence among the grieving. I suspect most of us doubt our worthiness for divine intervention. I know that my suffering is no greater than that of any parent who loses a child, and I am no more worthy of divine comfort than any other.

There is much I am unsure about, but I am sure about reality. The ache I feel every day is real. I keep wishing Jason could be with me. I want to watch him mature; I want to see what kind of an adult he becomes. Just before he died, Jason admitted that he had started listening to some of my records and liked much of the music from the late 1960's performed by Paul Simon, Jimi Hendrix, Carole King, Eric Clapton. Since his death I have listened to his tapes and I have learned to like some of the music he enjoyed such as Robert Palmer, Yellowjacket, Wang Chung, Gypsy Kings. I want to talk to Jason about this music, and about the books he's reading, the ideas he's puzzling over, his plans for next year. I wanted him to develop a closer relationship with his sister. The two of them had played out the sibling rivalry game, and I think Jason was ready to play the part of the wise big brother, the counselor and confidante. He would have done it well. He thought he had plenty of time. Now Tess will never get to experience such a relationship. He waited too long.

I have been thinking about an episode from the television series "Twilight Zone" which was one of Jason's favorites. The episode was about time travel. The groups of people from the future who engage in this recreational activity are given strict instructions not to stray from a specially constructed "path" because if they destroy or change anything in the past it could have disastrous consequences for the future. One man does stray from the path, but it appears that there is no damage. The group returns to their own time, and are dismayed to discover that it has been altered significantly for the worse. The leader believes the cause is related to their recent journey. The man who strayed from the path is accused and interrogated again. In the end, the man takes off his shoe and finds a crushed butterfly on his sole.

Perhaps Jason liked the show because he wanted to believe that every person was of some significance in life, including him. One of his favorite films was "It's a Wonderful Life" which is clearly a parable for that principle, but if he believed this why didn't he act on that belief? Why didn't he guard his life more carefully? Why wasn't he more alert to danger? I know his death will affect the future. Whether or not he achieved his dream of making movies, Jason would have been a positive force in the world. People would have benefitted from knowing him. Now that possibility is gone.

We influence the people we meet at work, the people who become our friends, the person we marry, the children we raise. Each of us is like that butterfly. We should think of ourselves as one of a few survivors of an endangered species. Even the skeptics in science have had to acknowledge this truth. In 1961, meteorologist Edward Lorenz, using computer simulations of weather, discovered that minor deviations in weather conditions (as compared to a previous set of conditions) will result in the development of significantly different weather patterns. This was not supposed to happen, and it was not welcome news to those whose job is to predict the weather. The technical term for Lorenz's discovery was "sensitive dependence on initial conditions." [18] It is an interesting coincidence that the informal term which scientists use in discussing this phenomenon is "the Butterfly Effect."

I liked many of the idealistic slogans of the 1960s, but I did not like "Today is the first day of the rest of your life." It is such an adolescent notion, implying no need to be concerned about what you do today because there are many days to come. This is not always true. It would be better to act as though today was the last day of your life. Such a belief would challenge you to establish your priorities, to question the purpose of your life, to consider how people would remember you after you die, to wonder what meaning your life will have for the people who knew you. Some might argue that they do not care how they are remembered. If so, then that will be part of the meaning of their life.

In the movie "Dead Poet's Society," the teacher said that life was a poem and each of us is invited to write a verse. What will that verse say? Newpaper obituaries only give us names and dates. Why don't they speak of the person who died. What was he like? What did she do? What did their life mean to their friends and neighbors and family?

When I have visited Jason's grave at the cemetery, I see so many monuments with no more than names and dates on them—a vast field of stone with blank spaces, the mute voices of the dead. What did life mean to them? What did they learn? What did they dream? Why didn't they tell us on the stone placed over them? It was their last chance to say something. At the head of Jason's grave is the family monument with his picture on it. Above his picture is the line from Keillor's essay, "when you look at the stars, you don't think small." Below his picture is the business card he designed for his imaginary film company and his company's slogan—"films for fun, not for profit." It's not much, but it's something. It suggests a life filled with dreams and plans. It suggests that dreams and plans are worth more than money. It is a thought worthy of a gravestone.

At the beginning of this chapter I quoted a verse once popular on tombstones and now I have come full circle to another epitaph, but there have been many questions in between and all of them are ultimately founded on one—does God exist? It has been many years since I reached the conclusion that this question could not be answered, so I would simply live life as morally as I could. I would try to be clear about my commitments and consistent in my actions. I would be grateful for each day given me and I would use my time to play a meaningful part in human progress. The reason for living such a life was not because it might result in a reward after death, but because it represented a satisfying way to live. When I died there would be nothing or something, but I could not do anything about that. If there was a life after death determined by divine judgment, I would trust that my life would be met with divine approval in some small measure. It was a reasonable resolution.

This resolution was rooted in much of the literature I have loved and the experiences I have had. One of my favorite poems from childhood was "Abou Ben Adhem" by Leigh Hunt [19]. An angel comes to Abou Ben Adhem in a dream holding a scroll in his hand where he is writing the names of those who loved the Lord. Abou asks if his name is there and the angel (apparently being of Christian persuasion) said it was not. Abou is sad for a moment, but smiles as he asks the angel to write that he is one who loves his fellow man. The angel writes and disappears. The next night the angel returns in another dream carrying another scroll which contains the names of those whom the Lord has blessed—"And lo, Ben Adhem's name lead all the rest" [19, p. 334]. I liked the God of that poem. I always thought this was a God you could love.

It was much harder to love the God of the world I lived in, especially when many of the people who claimed this God as their own were often so judgmental toward others, so arrogant in their faith, so insufferable in their self-righteousness. It seemed reasonable to ignore the question of God's existence and to let it be resolved at my death, but Jason's death shattered such a reasonable approach. I was left with fragments, pieces, random events. I was no longer content with being merely reasonable. I wanted some answers.

When I first started writing about Jason I remembered the biblical passage concerning the fall of a sparrow, so I looked for the quote in my King James Bible. It did not have the wording I wanted. I looked in other translations to find the one with the "right" words, and I found them in the "Good News Bible" which said "not one sparrow falls to the ground without your Father's *consent*" (my emphasis). I wanted to make God responsible. Although I refused to believe in a God who would intentionally maim and murder human beings, an omniscient God would have to be implicated in whatever evil occurs on earth. An omnipotent God could prevent evil and must at least "consent" to the evil that is done (as suggested by the opening chapter of the book of Job). If God existed, then God must have consented to Jason's death and I wanted to know why!

I still do not have answers, but I have tried to think about the question. A consequence of such thinking was my decision to use the King James translation in the quotation in the Prologue to this book. I did not want to blame God. That was too easy. Sometime later I was told that the King James rendition of this passage was probably the most accurate translation from the Greek. The translation did not refer to God as a monarch "consenting" to the fall of a lowly sparrow, but suggested that God falls with the sparrow, that God suffers with us. This made more sense to me, and this was a God I could accept. This God was not responsible for Jason's death; Jason was. For a moment of carelessness he paid the highest price. It has happened before. It will happen again.

That thought did not console me, but the Biblical passage offered consolation. It suggested that we do not pass into oblivion like a stone cast into the ocean, to be swallowed up with barely a ripple to testify to our passing. Each human life matters to God. This was the point of the gospel song which Garrison Keillor sang during the "sound check" before the benefit:

> I sing because I'm happy.
> I sing because I'm free.
> His eye is on the sparrow,
> And I know He's watching me. [16]

Is this "true"? I don't know. I do know that I am a religious person, if religious is defined as the effort to act consistently with one's deeply held values; however I have never regarded myself as a spiritual person. To be spiritual requires an ability to transcend conventional reality and enter another kind of reality, to participate in an alternate vision of life. If I was more spiritual perhaps I could resolve my doubts. Mystics and certain poets have tried to explain this transcendence, often suggesting that being spiritual is possible for everyone. I have read some of their books; they have been interesting but rarely coherent. I have not been able to understand this process of becoming spiritual.

While driving to a conference a few months after Jason's death, I decided to listen to some music. I selected a John Lennon tape which had belonged to Jason. I was watching the road and thinking about Jason, not paying attention to the music, until I heard one particular verse:

> "Love is asking
>   to be loved." [20]

I began to weep and I did not know why. I thought about some of the events that had happened since Jason's death: my prayer before the funeral, the door bursting open during the funeral, my prayer for help followed by the dream which purged me of my depression. I thought about the verse from Matthew beginning "Ask and it shall be answered," which insistently intruded into my consciousness prior to both prayers. It occurred to me that while I was asking for help, God was asking for love. Not demanding but asking. Perhaps God was willing to help me regardless of whether or not I gave my love in return, simply because I had asked. In helping me, God was offering love and consolation. How could I take all of that and not return love?

I had never asked God to love me, and I had not felt a need for God's love. With Jason's death I had become more vulnerable than ever before, and desperately in need of help. When I asked, I was answered. Since I am not a spiritual man, writing these words brings on nagging doubts and I imagine voices saying "coincidence" or "irrational" or "supernatural" or "superstition." Some of these voices are not imaginary; they are the voices of friends and even family. I want to transcend these voices. I want to develop a faith based not on reason but on love, based not on empirical evidence but on feeling. This will not be easy. A fledgling faith is a fragile creature and can fall as easily as the sparrow, but I will try to make it fly, and I will ask for help, and I will believe that my asking will be answered.

Remembering to Say Goodbye...

EPILOGUE
Father and Son

For this, for everything, we are out of tune;
It moves us not,—Great God! I'd rather be
A Pagan suckled in a creed outworn;
So might I, standing on this pleasant lea,
Have glimpses that would make me less forlorn;
Have sight of Proteus rising from the sea;
Or hear old Triton blow his wreathed horn. [21, p. 101]

William Wordsworth
"The World Is Too Much with Us"

What sort of faith do I hope to develop? Will it be a Christian faith? Probably not. Certainly not in the sense of a conventional Christian faith. I admire Christ's call for love and compassion and hope, so I will accept that as a contribution to my understanding of, and faith in, God. I will also borrow from American Indians. I respect their sense of the sacredness of life, the presence of life in all things. In the novel, *Little Big Man,* Thomas Berger accurately portrays this belief in a comment made by Old Lodge Skins, a leader of the Cheyenne (who call themselves "Human Beings"), "The Human Beings believe that everything is alive: not only men and animals but also water and earth and stones . . . But white men believe that everything is dead: stones, earth, animals, and people, even their own people. And if, in spite of that, things persist in trying to live, white men will rub them out" [22, pp. 227-228].

Perhaps I can become a "human being." I don't want to be "out of tune" with the wonder of the world. I want to believe in a universe animated by spiritual forces whispering holy truths to ears awake to hear. I want to walk in the world of miracles celebrated by Walt

163

Whitman, "To me every hour of the light and dark is a miracle,/ Every cubic inch of space is a miracle,/ Every square yard of the surface of the earth is spread with the same" [23, p. 313]. This will be no simple task, nor will the result be a state of shallow happiness. If I am open to the miracle of life, then the meaning of any death is that the world is diminished, and the suffering of multitudes must create sympathetic suffering in my soul. But suffering must be balanced with joy, which, if achieved, should result in a sense of reconciliation to the endless cycle birth and death. I had started down that path before Jason's death. Perhaps the best starting point is to return there and continue the journey.

As I write this epilogue, I am sitting in Jason's room, listening to some of the music he loved and wondering where he is, or if he is. I have moments of vivid recollection when Jason lives again, for me. It can happen when I listen to his favorite music or look at a photograph. On a concrete level, I can look around this room and see a few of Jason's movie posters on the walls, a few books he had read or intended to read, a few videotapes of his favorite films, a few photographs. Some of Jason's possessions are here: the Opus doll with the graduation cap and a red and blue striped tie, his Indiana Jones hat, and Casey—his Cabbage Patch doll. Out of sight, in a drawer, are the handwritten drafts of his poetry.

Cultures and religions around the world agree that there is some form of afterlife. Does this prove the truth of such beliefs or is it testimony to human fear and anxiety? Some believe only in the immortality of the genetic heritage we give our children to be passed on to their children and so on. In a sexist society that becomes even more narrowly defined as the birth of sons. I used to tease Jason about being the "last of the line." My paternal grandfather had two sons and one daughter, but my uncle never married and my father had three daughters and me. Since I had one daughter and one son, I told Jason he must marry and have lots of sons or there would be no one left in our branch of the Koppelman family tree to perpetuate the name. And now it has come to that.

At one time this actually might have bothered me. It is obviously a concern for some people. I read a newspaper article about a woman who not only kept her name after marrying, but wanted her children to take her last name because she was an only child and the last child in her branch of the family. Although her husband supported the decision, she encountered legal opposition. I remembered this incident because I was surprised by the blatant sexism inherent in this legal objection to a decision mutually agreed upon by a wife and husband. Prolonging a particular branch of a particular family name is of little importance to me.

If Jason had lived and never fathered children, I still would have enjoyed watching him grow and change. I would have applauded his successes, consoled him during defeats and advised him in times of uncertainty for as long as he wanted or needed such support. I will do the same for my daughter. It doesn't concern me whether she perpetuates my "genetic heritage." If she has children, it should be because she wants to have children. My main concern is for her to have a full life. I want her to do things which are important to her, to take necessary risks but avoid unnecessary ones, to experience and celebrate the joy of life.

Thinking about the end of a family line reminded me of *Buddenbrooks* by Thomas Mann [24]. After describing the family's rise to wealth and status, Mann focusses on Thomas Buddenbrooks. Although Thomas brings his family to the height of their success, his only brother has no children and Thomas has only one frail son who dies during childhood. Thus ends the highly respected Buddenbrooks family. Near the end of the book, Thomas meditates on death, and in that moment he has a fleeting experience of transcendental awareness:

> What *was* death? The answer came . . . he felt it within him, he possessed it. Death was a joy, so great, so deep that it could be dreamed of only in moments of revelation like the present. It was the return from an unspeakably painful wandering, the correction of a grave mistake, the loosening of chains, the opening of doors—it put right again a lamentable mischance.
> End, dissolution! These were pitiable words . . . What would end, what would dissolve? Why, this his body, this heavy, faulty, hateful incumbrance, which *prevented him from being something other and better*. [24, p. 526]

The "opening door" brought back memories of Jason's funeral. Is death simply a door opening to another form of existence? Is death the threshhold through which the soul must pass to enter another reality? Do we transcend? Are we transformed? I have often read passages in prose and poetry expressing such beliefs. I would like to believe. Garrison Keillor wrote about an insect flying into his mouth, forcing him to swallow. This "accident" transformed the insect into protein, "And so shall we all be changed someday." I would like to believe a transformation of some kind takes place. I also want to believe e. e. cummings when he writes:

> for life's not a paragraph
> And death i think is no parenthesis [25, p. 76]

I would like to believe this, but developing a faith does not necessarily lead to a belief in life after death. I have seen death. It was very real and seemed very permanent. I have had hints that something survives the death of the body, but it is difficult for hints to withstand the evidence of our senses which overwhelmingly tells us that dead is dead. A belief in life after death could be regarded as a desperate exercise in wish-fulfillment.

Like many people I demand too much. I want assurance; I want guarantees. During my undergraduate years I once talked to a student who claimed he was going to heaven after he died. When I suggested that a Christian should believe this was a decision only God could make, he insisted there was no doubt because he had accepted Jesus Christ as his personal Savior. I wonder if he ever developed a genuine faith because he obviously did not have one at this time. What he had (and apparently wanted) was certainty, and certainty has little to do with faith. Faith, by definition, means choosing to believe in the context of doubt and uncertainty. The dictionaries define it as choosing to believe "without proof."

I have heard such certainties expressed by many people professing to hold a Christian "faith." They claim that their certainty is based on the Bible, that the New Testament is all the proof they need. I have never understood how they can overlook what their "personal Savior" said about belief, belief based on faith, belief "without proof." This message was dramatically demonstrated in the account of one of the last appearances Christ made after the resurrection. According to Luke, Thomas had said he would not believe in the resurrection until he had seen Jesus and touched His wounds. When Jesus appears the doubting Thomas sees Him and touches His wounds, and only then does Thomas believe in the miracle. At that point Jesus blesses those who "have not seen and yet believe." It seems clear that Jesus is addressing the issue of faith, to refrain from demanding "proof," to choose to believe "without proof."

I am reminded of "Mr. Andrews," a short story by E. M. Forster [26]. The souls of a Christian and a Muslim are ascending to heaven and they converse to pass the time. Both regard the other as a heathen, but develop a strong sympathy for the other when suddenly they find themselves at the gate of heaven. Instead of requesting permission to enter, both of them plead for the admission of the other. Both are allowed inside, but are separated in order to partake of the particular version of heaven each expects to find: winged angels, gleaming halos and golden harps for the Christian; comfortable couches, luxurious clothes and virtuous virgins for the Muslim. The two souls meet again and both confess to feeling no profound sense of satisfaction with eternal life. They agree that their one moment of bliss occurred at heaven's portal when each pleaded for the admission of the other. Because of this, they decide to merge into the "world soul" which is outside the gates of heaven. They enter together "and they, and all the experiences they had gained, and all the love and wisdom they had generated, passed into it, and made it better" [26, p. 90].

If something survives the body's death, what is the nature of that survival? I find some comfort in Forster's suggestion that one's beliefs can influence one's experience of afterlife. French philosopher Blaise Pascal argued that since there was no objective way to prove or disprove the existence of an immortal soul, it is mathematically correct to claim a fifty-fifty chance for its existence [27]. If such a soul does not exist and death is final, then believing in an immortal soul makes little difference. But what if an immortal soul exists? Not believing in the soul could have adverse consequences whereas believing should have positive consequences. Pascal was trying to provide a logical reason for advocating an illogical belief.

Why not believe in a soul which survives the death of the body? Why not believe "without proof?" It is difficult because such a belief defies the evidence of our senses and the limits of our rationality. I once saw a poster that said "Having abandoned the search for truth, I'm looking for a really good fantasy." I believe in pursuing truth where it can be known, but when confronted with a question for which proof is not possible, why not choose a belief that gives hope and comfort? Why not believe that something survives the death of the body? Why not even believe that your belief can influence the nature of your existence after death? If this proves to be a fantasy, at least it is a good one, and a harmless one.

Our friends Ray and Sue visited us a few months after Jason's accident. During one of our conversations, I told Ray that I had been writing since Jason's accident as a form of therapy, and that I was thinking of revising and expanding these notes into a book. I said I already had a title. I would call it *The Fall of a Sparrow*. Ray audibly groaned, and I thought it was a reaction to the title. After some hesitation, he explained. His response had to do with an incident that happened when he and Sue were driving up for Jason's funeral.

> I drove onto a county road which would take me to the main U.S. highway north. Many birds were swarming out of the morning mist. I wondered if there were more than usual or if I was noticing the countryside teeming with life because of its contrast to the purpose of our trip. Suddenly we heard—"smack," "smack," smack!" A flock had burst out of the roadside foliage and hit our windshield. Birds flying into the car's grill happened often enough, but this was the first time I'd ever experienced them hitting the windshield. In fact, I'd never heard of them hitting the windshield. Sue was very upset. I said nothing. It was hard to ignore the incident because bloody feathers were stuck in the windshield-wiper blades on Sue's side.
>
> Smack! Smack! Smack! More birds hit the windshield. I heard a wail of pain from Sue. I saw a circle of blood the size of a quarter on the windshield directly in front of her eyes. In anguish Sue said, "That's what happened to Jason," and began sobbing. We finally came to a little town where I looked for a gas station to wash the blood and feathers off the windshield. A happy-looking shaggy dog trotted mindlessly into the path of our car and I had to brake hard to miss him. When we finally found a gas station and cleaned the windshield, Sue and I were both shaking.

Although raised as a Catholic, Ray no longer believes in any particular religion, and he prides himself on being rational and analytical. When he told me the story it was simply an example of a strange and painful coincidence which he had experienced. He rejects superstition and supernatural explanations for extraordinary events. He believes that all we have is our bodies and our minds and when those are gone there is nothing left. Such a belief requires one to accept that when my son's skull was smashed and his heart stopped, Jason ceased to exist. We buried the body and that was the end of it. I understand this belief, and I respect it as a rational conclusion, but I cannot accept it.

I don't know what constitutes human life, but I have always suspected that a human being is more than a marvelous machine, more than an efficient heart pump and a complex brain structure. Wondrous as those mechanisms are, we are more than the sum of their parts. To believe this is to believe in the possibility of miracles, but why not? If we believed in the possibility of miracles, we might recognize them when they happen.

I had a dream five years before Jason's death, another of those strange but vivid dreams which I rarely have. Jan and Jason and I were walking along an ice covered highway. Snow and ice surrounded us. In the distance behind us we could see snow covered hills. The straight road stretched on as far as the eye could see. It was cold. We were numb and miserable. At one point in the road there seemed to be a steep ditch on the left side. I walked over to look. As I neared the edge of the road, I could see that it was a sheer drop, and far below I could see a fertile field of lush, green grass. It was more beautiful than a summer meadow; it was like looking at the Elysian Fields.

I knelt down on my hands and knees as if drawn by a siren's song to lower myself over the edge and let myself fall to the field below. I remember thinking that if I hung down by my hands and then let go I might be able to land safely, even though my rational side said such a fall would be fatal. Despite the risk, I felt compelled to try. As I hung by my hands preparing to let go, I saw Tess out of the corner of my eye. There was a ledge jutting out from the cliff about five feet below the edge of the road and only a few feet to my left. The ledge was covered with green grass and even a few flowers, and Tess was dancing on it. I watched her dance and I felt her joy and I suddenly knew that I couldn't leave her. I started to swing my left foot over to her ledge so I could step up on it and climb back onto the road. Then I woke up.

This was another dream that seemed to be a warning, but once again I could not understand it. Although I claim no expertise in dream interpretation, I recall reading that ice and snow are symbolic of death, but I had no idea whose death was being foreshadowed in this dream. I did not try to analyze the dream. I did not think it was worth the effort. I did not believe in miracles. I assumed it was simply a complicated means by which my brain provided a sense of relief for some specific fear or in response to undefined anxiety. If I had believed in miracles I would have taken the trouble to understand the message. If I had understood the message, I could have warned Jason that he was in danger, that he must be especially careful. Would it have made a difference? Probably not. Jason would also have had to believe in miracles. And no one can be vigilant all of the time.

The message I can take from the dream is to pay attention, to recognize miracles, to be "in tune" with what is wondrous in the world, to cherish the (divine) spirit manifest in the dream image of Tess dancing on the ledge or the real image of Jason dancing in his room. Does that spirit survive the body's death? That would be a wonder, a miracle.

David Morrell wrote about miracles in *Fireflies* [28]. After his fifteen year old son died, David had a miraculous moment in his bedroom when he saw fireflies and heard his son's voice coming from one of them saying, ". . . I don't hurt anymore. I'm at peace. I'm where I belong. I'm okay" [28, p. 35]. Another miracle occurred during the service in a chapel at the mausoleum. A mourning dove which had been trapped in the locked chapel allowed David to pick him up and carry him outside. When David opened his hands to release the dove, it remained in the palm of his hands. After fifteen seconds passed, David worried that he had injured the bird when he picked it up, but the moment this thought occurred to him, the dove flapped its wings and flew. And he knew it was his son saying goodbye. For most of his adult life David Morrell had described himself as an agnostic. He admits he can be an agnostic no longer. He has been a witness of miracles.

I have read about cultures and religions around the world which have promoted a belief in something that transcends our mortal flesh. I have read the works of prophets and poets who have passionately promoted this belief. Such universal unanimity of opinion could be a compelling argument were it not for the attempts to describe the nature of our immortality. Catholics created the trinity of Hell-Purgatory-Heaven while Hindus and Buddhists developed elaborate reincarnation schemes. Such visions seem connected to flesh and blood and ego and not to a divine spirit. They are not transcendent. I am more comfortable with Walt Whitman's assertion that to die "is different from what anyone supposed, and luckier" [6].

Do I believe that? I want to believe it. I wonder what Jason believed. He didn't like talking about death. Although I read Bible stories to Jason when he was a child, I told him he had the right to choose to believe or not. As an adolescent, he claimed to be an atheist, but it was a flippant claim founded on an adolescent belief that he would live forever. If God is omniscient, then God knows what is in a person's heart and forgives what comes from the lips. I have met people full of caring words and empty of compassion. Like the hypocritical Pharisees, they only worry about appearances to disguise the corruption inside. Jason was a good person. He was kind and gentle and caring. He was not without flaws. None of us are. He was an ordinary person who might have made only modest achievements by societal standards, but he could have made important contributions to the people whose lives he might have touched. That is the possibility that exists for every human being.

As for believing in immortality, it is simply a matter of choice. I can choose not to believe in a life after death or to have some vague belief or adopt one of the many specific ones which have been developed. I want to believe in an immortality which will allow me to be with Jason and with others who are dear to me. Although my doubts persist, I believe something survives the death of the body. According to Luke, one of the two thieves crucified with Christ admitted deserving such punishment but said Jesus did not, and he asked to be remembered when Christ entered "thy Kingdom." I want to believe in the promise given to this flawed believer:

"Today, shalt thou be with me in paradise." [29]

My vision of paradise is simple. It is to see my son again, to tell him how much I missed him, to tell him how much I love him. I want to believe that such a vision will be fulfilled in the future. But not today. Today is Sunday. Today is also Father's Day. I have already opened my gifts and expressed my gratitude and embraced my wife and daughter. In the midst of their love and affection, I felt the pain of Jason's absence. I tried not to show it. I did not want my family to think I was not grateful for their gifts, or that Jason's death has distracted me from being able to love and appreciate them.

Father's Day. Simple questions occur to me. What should I say now when people ask me about my children? Should I speak only of Tess? I don't want to deny Jason's existence. If asked, I will acknowledge my son as well as my daughter, simply adding that my son was killed in a car accident when he was nineteen. This might make some people feel awkward, but I cannot allow their discomfort to make me neglect the memory of my son. In a sense, I can keep Jason alive as long as I live by remembering him, and sharing these memories with others. It is the only form of immortality I can give him, but I will give him that. It is one way to express my love for him. I cannot adequately explain how important this is to me, but e.e. cummings has perhaps suggested how I feel in the final verses of a poem:

here is the deepest secret nobody knows
(here is the root of the root and the bud of the bud
and the sky of the sky of a tree called life; which grows
higher than soul can hope or mind can hide)
and this is the wonder that's keeping the stars apart

i carry your heart (i carry it in my heart) [30, p. 156]

A Collection of Writing by Jason David Koppelman

To the stars who watch
as sparrows fall

Note: The following are excerpts from the journal Jason kept for his trip to England during the summer of 1987. After the trip he spent three weeks in Germany, but Jason did not have a good time there and wrote little about it.

6/30 — (On the bus on the way to Chicago) Great idea for a movie. Far in the future all forms of self expression are controlled, especially film because of its use in foreign propaganda; however a renegade production company managed to stay afloat and keeps making films. The government constantly sabotages these films making production very difficult, but the renegades are massing their own force to strike back.

7/1 — I feel ridiculous. Why am I crying? I know the answer why. I need their photo . . . of my parents. It just suddenly hit me that I don't have a picture of my mom and dad and for that matter of Tess either. I miss them so badly that it hurts. Being in the group, I didn't really notice anything. But now I'm just sitting here in my room trying to fall asleep and not being able to because I keep thinking of them. I need a picture. I'll have to write to them.

7/3 — Today was really quite hectic. We had concerts at two local schools today in Preston. All the children were quite excited. We had to give autographs to all of them. They thought we were celebrities or something. Some of the girls took the boys in the band, including me, by surprise by running up and hugging us while their friends took pictures. The boys had us sign their _arms_ and their bags. The girls were more conventional. That night we went to a pub called Gerschwins. I thought it was boring and the beer tasted terrible, so Shawn and I went for a walk on the boardwalk. We came across some other band members, both English and American. We got up a game of soccer. That was ***GREAT!***

7/4 — Today we went to Blackpool (England's Atlantic City) where we had two concerts. One was at Pleasure Beach which is an amusement park. The rides were all pretty average; stuff you'd find at Oktoberfest in La Crosse . . . The night concert was great. The conductor had me stand up after "Stars & Stripes" for my cymbal playing. I got many compliments.

7/6 — We travelled to Warwick castle. That was great except I got shin splints climbing Guy (?) Tower—450 steps: Ouch! The castle is owned by Madame Toussad's, so they had a nice exhibit. Next we went to Anne Hathaway's cottage which I enjoyed. I bought several things at the gift shop.

7/7 — . . . we went to Oxford. It was awesome. Besides the college, they had loads of stores. I bought many things. Next we went to London on a bus tour. When we got to the dorm rooms I found out that my room was better than all the other rooms. It had more and better furniture. There was a whole wad of Blue Tak (putty for sticking posters on walls) in my room so I spruced it up a bit by hanging some of the posters and tapestries on the walls. It looks really cool.

7/8 — Today was the most incredible day of my life. Everything went beyond perfect. First we went to the Tower of London. I got to see the Crown Jewels which were incredible. There wasn't even a line. The vault doors to that place were 5 feet thick steel. Whoa! Next we saw Westminster Abbey (and then) we went to the Hard Rock Cafe. They had everything, from Jimi Hendrix's guitar to Jimmy Connor's '79 Wimbledon Tennis racquet . . . After waiting in line for twenty minutes (to buy some T-shirts, etc.), we were finally close to the front when a guy in a RATT polo shirt came up to me and some other kids. He told us he was in a hurry and had to get to a concert and asked us to get him two sweatshirts. I figured he was a roadie with RATT (rock band). Then he pulled out his wallet which had about $5000 in it. So then I figured he was a manager. I told him I'd get them for him, figuring he'd probably give me a little something extra. When I brought back the sweatshirts, he thanked me and pulled up a briefcase, opened it up and put them in. On the briefcase it said on a bumper sticker, "Billy Joel World Tour '87." Starting to sweat, I asked him if he was the manager of Ratt or something. He said no, but he was the manager of Billy Joel. By then I *freaked*! Then I asked him who the shirts were for and he said one was for him and the other was for "Bill"!!! So in other words, I bought Billy Joel a Hard Rock Cafe sweatshirt. I found out later that there was a Billy Joel concert that night at Wembley (?) Stadium and that he was planning on going to the Hard Rock Cafe later that evening. I just couldn't believe it. Oh, the manager only gave me a pound for my trouble. I didn't care about that though. Next I went to a Virgin Records Superstore. The place had three floors . . . To cap off a fabulous day, that night we saw the play "Les Miserables." That was astounding. Absolutely incredible. I bought a sweatshirt, a T-shirt and two programs and a poster! Well, I have one more buy to talk about—A goodbye, and good night.

7/16 — Sorry I haven't written in a while, but there hasn't been much of anything going on worth writing about. I'm in Germany now and I haven't seen anything special . . . I saw the movie "Platoon" last night with German dubbed in. I have to see "Platoon" again now in English so I can reassure myself of the voices and that it was a good film. Somehow, through the dubbing of German, it was transformed from an anti-war to a pro-war film. That is perverse. The walls of the theater "lobby" (I use the term loosely because it was more like a bar) were plastered with old movie posters. I happened to see an old German "Star Wars" poster. It was ruined of course. The theater itself was smaller than your average private screening room. Very small! Only twelve more days to go before I can leave this anti-movie *HELL.*

7/? — List of things I want to do when I get back—The night I get back I want to see the 9:00 p.m. show of InnerSpace, or something, get a large Rocky Rococco pizza and watch a movie on videotape. Thursday I want to play a lot of video games, basketball, go out on the river (on Jet Skis maybe or a boat), and have a barbeque by the river. For lunch tacos at Taco John's. I also want to borrow all of Matt's Billy Joel tapes. That night I want to see two more movies. And another videotape. After that I'm going to ad lib. But that's the beginning of a wonderful new life in America. A life I will appreciate for a long time.

KATE

I. She's not the loveliest girl
       I've ever seen,
       yet she has enticed me
       for eight years.
    We've rarely spoken,
       but I cherish the times we have.
    My eyes follow her in the halls,
       and my mind follows her everywhere
       else . . .

II. She is the wind
       and I am the tree.
    Whenever she is near,
       she rushes through my branches
       making them wave and quiver,
       but once she is gone
       I feel relaxed and remember:

    Not how tense she made me,
       but how pure and fresh the air was.

CONCESSION

The smell of butter
   clings to the air.

Popping popcorn
   drowns out the impatient crowd.

The soda machine whines
   trying to fill a bottomless cup.

Candy is set upon the counter
   and snatched away as quickly.

With candy in pocket,
   soda and popcorn in hand,
   the crowd disperses
   leaving only the sound
   of popcorn
   popping.

STORM

The wind is howling
I cannot sleep

A storm has come
  and lightning flashes
  disrupting first the darkness
  then the silence
  beyond my control
  or anyone's

The window is open
  and the falling rain
  is blown by the wind
  through my screen
  drizzling onto
  my body
  it tingles
  almost uncomfortably

    (almost)

Truly a unique experience
  but it escapes me
  as lightning cracks the sky
  again

How can this experience be enjoyed
  with the elements
  snapping at your senses
  ruining the moment
  of sheer sensation
    feeling
    learning

The agony of frustration
  of yearning for only the mist
  pure in itself
  but getting the ferocity of the storm
  in its place

My soul is howling
  and now I weep

I FLY

I Fly

my arms are outstretched
air blows through my fingers
my clothes ripple in the wind
below me are the troubles and
                    the problems
of the real world
i have escaped that place
everything is below me now
so i climb higher and higher
into the silence and isolation
of space

I Dream

i am motionless
my breath has ceased
my heart is still
my eyes open and i am awake
but i am met by disappointment
the sky that surrounded is gone
only to be replaced
by four constricting walls

I Attempt

one day
i will climb the highest building
my arms will reach outward
air will blow through my fingers
my clothes will ripple in the
                    wind
i am strong
fear no longer exists
so

I Jump

GOOD MORNING

The time this morn' is six o'clock.
I guide my dog along the walk.
The virgin snow that fell last night
is crushed beneath my feet with spite.
The wind is sharp, and I am cold.
The sky is dark, but I am bold.
My dog darts forth from tree to tree.
He's looking for a place to pee.

Then suddenly to my chagrin,
My dog is pissing on my shin!

THOUGHTS OF BEDTIME

Dorms are so lonesome at night,
The plain colored walls perpetuate
        the isolation.
The flannel sheets are my
Only reminder of home.
The posters on the walls are mine,
    as are the knickknacks on the desk,
    but it's not my walls or my desk,
Only between the sheets am I surrounded
        by home.

I close my eyes and hear my dad
    (he reads to me every night)
Telling tales of dwarves and goblins,
    rabbits and quests,
    space and the destiny of man.

"Please dad, read another chapter."
"What the hell are you talking about?"

My roommate has spoken,

    but I hear only the past
    as my dad gives me a kiss
    and tucks me in
        (between the flannel sheets)
    and wishes me goodnight.

RED ROUTE

I am turned sideways on the seat
    backed against a cold, smudged window;
    at each stop, less room remains for hopeful riders
        at upcoming stops.

I slide around in the seat in anticipation of
    weary workers with a desire to rest
        their feet;
    as usual, mine is the last vacant seat.

We're off for the next stop.

This used to be painful
    (like being picked last for the team)
but no more.
I've come to expect it now.
I've adapted to whatever it is about me
    that repulses people.

As the doors open, the herd of people
    outside begins to filter onto the bus.
Several people walk by this vacant seat,
Obviously preferring to stand than to sit by
    such a repulsive person.

Sometimes I wish to stand and ask . . . no,
    yell at this person —
"Why don't you sit?"
But I don't; it does not bother me
        (any more).

A girl sits next to me.
I only know because I saw her purse.
I am not allowed to look at her directly
    for it's not proper bus etiquette;
        so, I resort to staring blankly out the
            window.
It's dark, so all I see is my reflection
    distorted somewhat by the smudges.
I lean back slightly and notice that
    I can see the girl next to me
        in the window.

She is beautiful;
    her face is softened in the reflection
            glowing;
    her hair is pushed back over her ear,
      but a few strands remain
      resting on her cheek;
    her eyes glisten;
    she sits so close, almost as though
      she were leaning against my arm,
      resting and reassured.

My mind has carried me far
    (too far)
    for surely she is just tired and
    needed to sit;
    the bus has arrived at my stop; so,
      I stand and excuse myself as I
        pass by her;
    as I stand on the curb, the bus departs,
    leaving me in a diesel cloud
    wondering.

Yes

I wonder if she liked me.
I convince myself that this wondering
    is merely romantic silliness;

  so I turn,
  and head home,
  and forget.

ENCOUNTER

What is love,
but that which entrances our minds
    and our hearts
into believing that what is before us
is real rather than fantasy

It is this primary emotion
that drives us to delve deeper
into what sparks our imaginations.
It expands an instant into experience
to create an entirely new range of
    feeling.

What is love?

It is that initial fascination with beauty
and the encounter of life that results.

ENLIGHTENMENT

my corner of the room
is crowded in blackness
i crouch among shadows
awaiting help
where is it
my shirt is damp
tears falling from my chin
i can't stop crying

who am i kidding
i am not crying
but i want to so badly
to release some frustration
drop by drop
but can not
this frustrates me more
where is the help
that i need so badly
where are my tears
that beg to be set free

two hours blend into history
and still i sit
help has yet to arrive
and i doubt it ever will
i am abandoned again
waiting is death

so i stand to help myself
i must find the light
my hands paw the walls
for an answer
a guide
i find a switch at long last
light
my finger raises the switch
and the room flashes with light
a light so bright
that i am not able to see
so i wait for my eyes to adjust
but my stare is met with
infinite blackness

the bulb has burnt out
now
i can cry

A ROMANTIC TRILOGY

1

I stand alone in my corner of the room
    the band plays on . . . the tunes . . .
I think of being with you
    standing in the doorway . . .

Your face leaves me in awe . . .

    My heart has become

Lost in your eyes
    as your stare meets mine,
You walk across the floor,
    and our arms intertwine.
We sit at the table
    and I pour you some wine

    As the evening begins to unfold . . .

    As we chat

Many thoughts flash through my mind;
I hear wedding bells chime;
I believe now is the time
            to propose;
That question I spring,
As I unveil the engagement ring;
You hold it so gently, a smile it brings
      as you utter the simple word—"yes."
Yes, I can remember when candlelight flickered
      and gave off the glow of romance,
      and I can remember when "lovers" meant simply
      simply two people in love.

2

In the church we stand before the crowd,
      our hearts beating loud
      proclaiming our vows
To love and cherish all that we are
      together or afar . . .

Our love shines like
Stars in your eyes
      as I make a small wish
      that everything's perfect
      and nothing's amiss;
      you lean towards me slowly
      and softly we kiss
As the crowd explodes with applause . . .

Later, we finally are off by ourselves,
Knowing full well
      that our love is only
      a spell cast upon us, by powers above.
You can tell by our smiles what we're both thinking of;
      our passion is flaming as we're making love
      and the firelight fades to a glow . . .

Oh, I can remember when candlelight flickered
      and gave off the glow of romance,
      and I can remember when "lovers" meant simply
      simply two people in love.

#3

Time marches on and we now have a home,
a simple place to call our own,
but now we feel alone . . .
Inside, our love is still so fine
so why am I so blue?

Maybe I need something
    new in my life, like a change of scene.
I feel something's missing, how crazy that seems!
You are so perfect; you're all that I need,
    but you smile understandingly . .

You sit me down to say something to me;
(how special it must be)
    as you slowly
    reveal
    a small secret you've kept
    for a while.
"I've been to the doctor," you say with a smile.
It suddenly hits me; my eyes grow wide,
    knowing the joy of a father-to be . . .

Oh, I can remember when candlelight flickered
    and gave off the glow of romance,
    and I can remember when "lovers" meant simply
    simply two people in love.

PARENT

I was the father
    of two children
    each of a distinct
    character
    for fifteen years

I bathed in their
    excitement
    and intensity
    was fascinated
    by each style
    of innocence
One had innocence
    of the mind
    always dreaming
    thinking
    wondering
    and imagining
    things that were not
    my second
    had a physical innocence
    a small little person
    so fragile
    yet submissive

Both are the
    embodiment of purity
    and now one has died
    my second child
    has passed away
    and though it was foreseen
    i could not prepare for his loss.

His death
    left me hollow
    and uncomfortable with myself

I turned to my
    now only son
    and clung to him
    for fear that he too
    would leave
    but now

I can't let go
    and the innocence of the mind
        rules my life.

ENTRANCE ESSAY FOR VITERBO COLLEGE

In many ways, the family structure is very similar to that of our national government. We have an executive branch (the mom), the judicial branch (the dad), and the legislative branch (the entire family). It is in the legislative branch where the most bickering is found, because the children are actually allowed to express themselves. The most regular topic for bickering is the family chores and how they will be distributed.

The chores seem to be limited ("How much can there be in one small house?"), yet the judge and the executive always have more. Chores can be subdivided into three categories: yard work, housework, and repairs.

Through history, yard work has evolved into a father/son experience. The father, having many years under his belt, as well as a few beers in his belly, has taken on the easiest of the tasks—mowing. He rides the mower like a king, and rides slowly as he overlooks his offspring performing the more menial tasks that he has thrust upon them. The son(s) weed, rake, trim, prune, and sweep as their faces grow more numb from boredom with each passing task.

Housework has also evolved into a mother/daughter experience with the occasional, reluctant help from the father ("the sexist pig!"). What is interesting with housework is that everything seems to get done twice. The mother carefully assigns a task to each of her offspring, and then proceeds to do it over again to her own satisfaction.

*   *   *

Note: Going to England in 1987 apparently made Jason think of his possible death. He jotted down some notes in his diary which he called "A Brief Will of Jason Koppelman." Some excerpts:

All my soundtrack albums are to be given to Matt Schumann.

All exercise equipment of mine is to go to Chuck Sween.

My stereo and tapes are to be given to my sister.

To my parents I leave my small Star Wars poster and torn E.T. poster to remember me by.

All of my Star Wars "toys" in my closet are to be given to an orphanage or something like that.

If I die before 7/19/87, then I will have seen Star Wars 99 times. If after then 100.

Thank You, All. It was an interesting life.
Goodbye, Farewell, Amen.

A long time ago, in a galaxy far, far away . . .
. . . there was Jason

WITHOUT YOU

POSTSCRIPT: The following poem was written for Jason shortly after his fatal car accident on September 13, 1989 by his sister, Tess Elana Koppelman. It speaks for all of us.

The days go on;
The nights sleep on;
The clouds roll on;
The earth spins on.

Yet, I feel something missing.
My mind keeps insisting
That something's not right
On a night like tonight.

The grass grows on;
The flowers bud on;
The sun sets on;
The moon shines on.

I sit here saying
(Forever praying)
Dear God, I know
What is wrong.

The souls rise on;
The angels sing on;
The clock ticks on
As time goes on.

What is wrong is simple you see,
A part of my heart has been taken from me,
But I don't mind as I look at the stars,
For I know that this someone will never be far.

The children shall laugh on;
The adults shall work on;
The animals shall go on;
The flowers shall bloom on.

But only a lucky few
Can live on knowing
What it's like
Without you.

References

1. Matthew 10:29-31, *Holy Bible (King James Version)*, American Bible Society, New York. (Note: All biblical references are based on this edition of the Bible.)
2. Hugo, Victor, *The Laughing Man,* Bellina Phillips (trans.), The Rittenhouse Press, Philadelphia, Pennsylvania, Book IV, Chapter III, 1894.
3. Ferlinghetti, Lawrence, The World is Beautiful Place, *A Coney Island of the Mind,* New Directions Books, New York, 1958.
4. Pirandello, Luigi, War, *Great Modern European Short Stories,* Douglas and Sylvia Angus (eds.), Fawcett Publications, Inc., Greenwich, Connecticut, 1967.
5. Keillor, Garrison, Laying on Our Backs Looking Up at the Stars, *We Are Still Married: Stories and Letters,* Viking Press, New York, 1989.
6. Whitman, Walt, A Child Said "What is the grass?" *Leaves of Grass,* Bantam Books, New York, 1983.
7. Shakespeare, William, Hamlet (Act V, Scene II), *William Shakespeare: The Complete Works,* Alfred Harbage (ed.), Penguin Books, Baltimore, Maryland, 1969.
8. Crane, Stephen, A Man Said to the Universe, *The Collected Poems of Stephen Crane,* Wilson Follet (eds.), Knopf, New York, 1930.
9. Zweig, Stefan, Letter from an Unknown Woman, *Letter from an Unknown Woman* (motion picture), Virginia Wright Wexman (ed.), Rutgers films in print series, v. 5, Rutgers University Press, New Brunswick, New Jersey, 1986.
10. Frost, Robert, Out, Out . . ., *The Complete Poems of Robert Frost,* Holt, Rinehart and Winston, New York, 1958.
11. Anonymous, *Beowulf,* Burton Raffel (ed.), New American Library, New York, 1963.
12. Keiller, Garrison, Who Do You Think You Are?, *We Are Still Married: Stories and Letters,* Viking Press, New York, 1989.

13. Dickinson, Emily, Pain Has an Element of Blank, *Selected Poems and Letters of Emily Dickinson,* Robert Linscott (ed.), Doubleday Anchor Books, Garden City, New York, 1959.
14. Kipner, Steve and Parker, John, *Hard Habit to Break,* EMI Music Publishing Company and Music Corporation of America, New York, 1984.
15. Melville, Herman, *Moby Dick,* The Bobbs-Merrill Company, Inc., New York, 1964.
16. *His Eye is on the Sparrow,* words and music by Charles H. Gabriel, July Publishing Company, 1976.
17. Donne, John, Meditation 17, *The College Survey of English Literature,* Alexander M. Witherspoon (ed.), Harcourt, Brace & World, Inc., New York, 1951.
18. Gleick, James, The Butterfly Effect, *Chaos: Making a New Science,* Penguin Books, New York, 1987.
19. Hunt, Leigh, Abou Ben Adhem, *The Standard Book of British and American Verse,* Nella Braddy (ed.), The Garden City Publishing Company, Inc., Garden City, New York, 1932.
20. Lennon, John, *Love,* Sony Music, Nashville, Tennessee, 1970.
21. Wordsworth, William, The World is Too Much With Us, *Major British Writers,* G. B. Harrison (ed.), Harcourt, Brace & World, Inc., New York, 1959.
22. Berger, Thomas, *Little Big Man,* Fawcett Publishing, Inc., Greenwich, Connecticut, 1964.
23. Whitman, Walt, Miracles, *Leaves of Grass,* Bantam Books, New York, 1983.
24. Mann, Thomas, *Buddenbrooks,* H. T. Lowe-Porter (trans.), Vintage Books, New York, 1984.
25. cummings, e. e., since feeling is first, *a selection of poems,* Harcourt, Brace & World, Inc., New York, 1965.
26. Forster, C. S., Mr. Andrews, *75 Short Masterpieces: Stories from the World's Literature,* Roger B. Goodman (ed.), Bantam Books, New York, 1961.
27. Pascal, Blaise, *Pensees,* W. F. Trotter (trans.), E. P. Dutton & Company, Inc., New York, 1958
28. Morell, David, *Fireflies,* E. P. Dutton, New York, 1988.
29. Luke, Chapter 23, verse 43, *Holy Bible (King James Version),* American Bible Society, New York.
30. cummings, e. e., i carry your heart, *a selection of poems,* Harcourt, Brace & World, Inc., New York, 1965.